The Great Way West

The History and Romance of the Great Western Railway's Route from Paddington to Penzance

By David St John Thomas

David & Charles
from their head office at Newton Abbot railway station
also London · North Pomfret (Vt) · Vancouver

Publisher's note

This book is about a railway we know intimately. We look out upon it from our offices. We use it regularly to take us and our books to other parts of the country. It is also a railway for which we have much affection — not just the railway enthusiasts among us who enjoy retelling its colourful history, but those who enjoy the superb slice of English countryside through which it passes and the better-than-average trains and restaurant car service. If the book had a dedication it might be to the restaurant car crews, many of whom are our staff's friends.

Here we present a panorama of the line's history and scenery. When we started work on it, we were amazed by how many of the canals, other railways, historic houses, natural features and other things that can be seen from the train are subjects of David & Charles books or covered thoroughly in one or more of our general works. Without we hope making it look like an advertising gimmick, for there is a genuine partnership between the railway and ourselves, we have included a list of such books, which are also referred to at the appropriate point on the strip maps. The maps were drawn by our staff artist Vic Welch.

David St John Thomas

ISBN 0 7153 7063 4

Library of Congress Catalog Card Number 75-10530

© David & Charles 1975

Set in Univers
and printed in Great Britain at the Alden Press, Oxford
for David & Charles (Holdings) Limited South Devon House Newton Abbot Devon

Published in the United States of America
by David & Charles Inc North Pomfret Vermont 05053 USA

Published in Canada
by Douglas David & Charles Limited 132 Philip Avenue North Vancouver BC

The Great Way West

The Great Western route to Penzance: what thoughts it evokes! Trains that were more than a little different — famous, punctual, clean. Holidays, sunshine and cream, beautiful countryside and dramatic coast. The way back from America; the way out of London at times of evacuation. The Great Way West figures in the history of almost every family. It has a warm spot in the heart of millions, from royalty and writers to tourists and businessmen.

It is hard to know where to start. But though this is not a railway book in the narrowest sense — I hope it will be enjoyed by many people with just a general interest in the route and the countryside it serves — let us begin with the fabric of the railway itself.

For a start, then, the Great Western was a unique railway with a romance of its own that is now cemented in social as well as railway history. It was truly great and forward-looking in many things; mean, slow, conservative in many others. It was always different. It began by choosing a gauge different from that established by other railways. Its engineer, Isambard Kingdom Brunel, did not follow precedent easily — and indeed it has to be said that in the building of the Great Western and its extensions into Cornwall, he was forced to work out many calculations (such as those of stresses in bridges) that nobody had done before. He felt that the 'narrow' gauge of 4ft 8½in adopted by the Stockton & Darlington, Liverpool & Manchester and other early lines would be too constraining for his grand trains. So the 'broad' gauge of 7ft 0¼in was brought into being to give greater stability and allow more powerful locomotives to haul trains at greater speed.

A broad-gauge line that went straight over, under or through natural obstacles, the Great Western from Paddington to Bristol was magnificently engineered. Very little of the basic structure has been changed since, and the exit from Paddington is the least fussy and quickest of any from London's termini. During much of its history, it has carried the world's fastest trains, beginning with the *Flying Dutchman* in the late 1860s and continuing with the *Cheltenham Flyer* between the wars; it also carried, and still does, the *Cornish Riviera Express* or *Limited*, for many years making the longest non-stop journey in the world.

The line's locomotives have always been outstanding and different. The Great Western was built upon a happy partnership between Brunel and the locomotive man Daniel Gooch, whose majestic machines — some with driving wheels of 8ft in diameter — established a tradition of pride and pleasure that has not been entirely broken even today. The best locomotives on a well laid-out road meant good speeds even at the start of the railway age, and as speeds increased — the best trains almost always being quicker than those on other major routes — the West of England was steadily drawn into the national scheme of affairs. Previously more Cornishmen had travelled abroad to dig holes for precious minerals than had ever come to London, and such journeying as was done between the capital and the far west was mainly by slow and unreliable ship.

There was only one really bad period in the Great Western's history, at the end of the broad-gauge era when it had become obvious the company would have to conform with the national 'narrow' gauge to overcome the ever-greater operating problems caused by lack of uniformity — but Daniel Gooch, then superintendent of the line, had little heart for such transformation. Death saved him having to issue the final execution order. Though the broad-gauge's territory had been steadily whittled away, the final conversion of the main line between Exeter and Truro (Paddington-Exeter and Truro-Penzance were mixed three-rail tracks) and many branches in the West took place in May 1892, when an army of workers moved in from all parts of the system and one of the Great Western's legends of service was created. The tears flowed when the last broad trains passed; at Dawlish, passengers in the final down and up trains joined hands to sing 'Auld Lang Syne'.

In the last years broad-gauge coaches were made up to 10ft wide, and first-class passengers enjoyed exceptional spaciousness and lack of oscillation. But no corridor coaches or restaurant cars travelled on the broad gauge, all London trains making a compulsory ten-minute stop at Swindon for passengers to refresh themselves.

Restaurant cars, corridor coaches, steam heating, electric lighting and of course through trains from the midlands and north were part of the Great Western great awakening following the change of gauge. Hereafter the company remained in the forefront.

Even though the gauge had changed, many of the earlier traditions continued, and the new generation of locomotives showed their direct descent from the old. For the Great Western had permanence and prided itself on continuity — a characteristic that crept ever more to the fore. It was the only major railway to retain its identity in the 'grouping' of 1923, and the green locomotives and chocolate-and-cream coaches became loved as much for their historic associations as for any intrinsic value. Not that one should decry the locomotives in particular. Though the basic shape — notably the graceful tapering boiler — was maintained, and Castles followed on naturally from Stars, and then Kings from Castles, the machines were in fact the finest in the land. Occasionally critics asked when the Great Western would invent something really new, but they then had to admit that it was not really necessary. In fact the continuity was preserved even after nationalisation in 1947. For a period the Western Region was allowed to restore the time-honoured chocolate-and-cream livery for coaches of its named expresses (the number of named trains then grew rapidly), and thus in the late 1950s the *Cornish Riviera Express* looked little different from its predecessors of half a century before. Indeed the very same locomotives hauled it for over a quarter of a century.

This continuity helped the Great Western in its determination to assert its difference, and was loved. But all kinds of other efforts were made too. To the end (and still today where not replaced by the electronic breed) its signals clicked down rather than up to indicate all-clear. In the restaurant car you drank Great Western whisky and ate Huntley & Palmer's Great Western assorted biscuits. Posters, jig-saw puzzles and a succession of books for 'Boys of all Ages' made heroes of the trains and their crews. 'Smiling Somerset', 'Glorious Devon' and 'The Cornish Riviera' were invented and skilfully exploited into Britain's major holiday playground. Some resorts — Newquay is an excellent example — were veritable Great Western creations. Why go to Italy when Cornwall has such warmth and charm and the train journey there is such a delightful part of the holiday? That was the message behind a poster which included maps of Italy and a stretched Cornwall almost identical in shape.

It is the holiday associations that slip a warm glow into most people's feelings toward Paddington, as compared with other London termini. From around 1890 until the overseas package holidays of recent times, an amazing proportion of the British population took at least some of their holidays in the South West, and it was therefore natural that the country's best trains should be on this route. Paddington station and its facilities were substantially rebuilt between the wars, with peak holiday traffic to Devon and Cornwall in mind. Businessmen making day trips from the West to London were then unimportant compared with those going down for a stay beside the sea. Every signalman, guard and porter knew it was a special offence to delay the *Cornish Riviera* or *Torbay Express.*

The Great Western was helped by a route of infinite variety and beauty. 'Modern G.W.R. compartments are fitted with wide observation windows which afford extensive views without admitting dust or draught,' boasted a publication describing the route. 'The observant traveller notices, for instance, how the red soil of Devon appears immediately the county boundary is crossed, and how farmhouses, church towers and even footpath stiles differ in shape and material from county to county.' Above all, the trains actually passed beside the sea — in fact within feet of salt water for many miles, down the Exe estuary, along the sea wall between Dawlish and Teignmouth, and then up the Teign estuary. The sea wall is one of the route's many special features: it was difficult to build, has always been expensive to maintain, has been washed away on a number of occasions, and to this day gives gasps of pleasure. In a packed train from Yorkshire carrying families to their first post war holiday in 1945, the excitement among the children when the waves came into view was something many of the adults present still remember. The anger in the restaurant car of a train in the 1930s when a lady passenger insisted on drawing the blind at this particular spot because she feared the sun would fade the colours in her hat also lingers in at least one memory . . .

But there are plenty of outstanding things to see between Paddington, surely one of the most magnificent and practical monuments of early Victorian achievement, and Penzance's ugly station beside the water. You run beside the Wiltshire Downs and see several of their white horses. There are views of Dartmoor and Bodmin Moor. You strike the South Coast of Cornwall at two points and have a brief glimpse of the North Coast. There is a magnificent stretch of line beside the Kennet & Avon Canal and several other canals are seen as well as the Thames and most of the West Country's famous rivers. You see Exeter and Truro Cathedrals, the Isle of Avalon (where King Alfred allegedly burnt those cakes) and St Michael's Mount. Castles, tin mines, fishing villages, grand houses and farms of all types add to the interest. The railway itself supplies fine bridges and viaducts and Brunel's *pièce de résistance*, the Royal Albert Bridge, carrying the line high over the Tamar between Devon and Cornwall at Saltash. Much of England's, and especially the West Country's, history can be told and be seen on the ground in the course of the train journey: probably nowhere else in the western world is so much encompassed in so few miles.

In all, the route is only 305 miles; to Newton Abbot, where I normally alight, but 193, emphasising how much of the route is in the West itself. The very contrasts perhaps give the impression of greater distance, for certainly most Londoners regard Newton Abbot as further away than Liverpool, also 139 miles. Devon and Cornwall remain a different land. Their very difference can best be savoured from the Great Way West, so if your normal alighting point too is well short of Penzance I hope this book may encourage at least one trip to journey's end.

From Bradshaw's Railway Guide, 1844, shortly after the opening to Exeter

The Railway in the News

Paddington to Penzance is a route full of special episodes in railway history. It was on this line, for instance, that man first travelled at 100 miles an hour; or it would be fairer to say that so it was claimed, for sharp has been the controversy since. For several generations railwaymen gave special attention to the boat trains from Plymouth, passengers and mail being rushed by land to London and getting there a full day earlier than if they had stayed aboard ship into Southampton. In the early years of the century there was keen competition between the Great Western and the London & South Western, speeds steadily increasing by both routes. In 1904 the 4-4-0 locomotive *City of Truro* was at the head of a train of five big eight-wheeled vans of mail, and according to a railway expert who happened to be travelling on the train reached a speed of 102.3 miles an hour descending Wellington Bank. No announcement was made at the time for fear of frightening the public, and when the record was published in *The Railway Magazine* some people denied it was possible. To this day Western men believe it and others doubt it.

What was obvious was that very high speeds were being attained. *City of Truro* maintained an average of 70.2 miles an hour between Exeter and Bristol on that occasion, and the engine which replaced her at Bristol, a 7ft 8in single driver, averaged 71.5 thence to Paddington. Inclusive of the Bristol stop, it only took from 9.23am to 1.09pm to travel the Great Way Round from Plymouth via Bristol to Paddington.

Two years later an ocean express of the South Western was derailed at high speed in Salisbury, with terrible loss of life. This prematurely ended competition in speed before the opening of the Great Western's shorter route via Castle Cary in 1906. Though enjoying a monopoly of ocean traffic in later years, the Great Western continued to treat it with reverence. The ocean terminal at Plymouth, though now a mile from the nearest rail, was handsomely rebuilt after World War II, and it was also in postwar years that Castle class locomotive *Isambard Kingdom Brunel* (an appropriate choice) traversed the 227½ miles to Paddington in the all-time record of 3 hours and 37 minutes.

Despite high-speed running since the days of the *Flying Dutchman* of the 1860s, the Great Way West has been a singularly safe route, no passenger ever being killed in a train accident anywhere west of Norton Fitzwarren, near Taunton. Nor were there any accidents of note elsewhere on the route between the two Norton Fitzwarren disasters killing 10 and 27 passengers respectively, just half a century apart, in 1890 and 1940. Freight accidents happen on any hilly route and in its early days the Cornwall Railway's trains had a special propensity to run off the track, one locomotive ending funnel-down in the mud of a tidal creek. But the Cornwall Railway's most famous accident, a head-on crash between two goods near Menheniot, was caused, simply, by the wrong Dick starting up his train when the signalman shouted 'Right away, Dick'.

That the Great Western was probably the safest railway in the world was due both to its pioneering of automatic train control (audible signals being sounded in the cab and the brake being applied if the driver did not take appropriate action) and to the high standard of track maintenance. With exceptions, such as the named saloons on ocean specials and the 1935 'Centenary Stock' of the world's longest non-stop express, the *Cornish Riviera* — and even that would not seem particularly comfortable by today's standards — rolling stock was not outstanding. The most comfortable ride in Britain was on an LMS coach travelling on the GW, it was said! Much of the rolling stock was incidentally given routine maintenance at Newton Abbot in sheds now converted into the warehouse of the publishers of this book. It was immediately after the 'Atmospheric Caper' that Newton Abbot assumed its role as locomotive headquarters for the South West, many of the South Devon Railway's broad-gauge locomotives actually being built in this mini-Swindon.

The story of the Atmospheric Caper has been told many times. Brunel was in fact backing the precursor of electrification, applying power made in stationary power-houses as an alternative to locomotives. The theoretic advantage was great, since different rates of power could be supplied by the stationary engine houses according to the local gradients — as opposed to having to stop a train to add an extra engine to help it over a hill, or provide an unnecessarily powerful engine on the flatter parts of the route.

These engine houses, extraordinary buildings, one beside the track at Starcross and another at Torre still surviving, pumped out the air from a pipe laid between the rails. A piston travelled inside this pipe, being connected to the leading coach — or the piston carriage — through a continuous hinged longitudinal valve, opened and closed on the zip-fastener principle; air let in behind chasing the vacuum in front pulled the train. When the contraption was in order, speeds of up to 60 miles an hour were attained, and the lack of smoke and dirt did something to soothe the irritation of the railway's incredible egotism in laying itself between Dawlish's Lawn and beach. But technical troubles are not peculiar to our own generation. Everything had to be learned, and time and money ran out. The longitudinal valve gave especial problems, though there is little backing for the local legend that it was rats chewing it that caused the trouble. Atmospheric trains lasted only about a year, running first from Exeter to Teignmouth and then for a few months on to Newton Abbot.

The experiment cost the South Devon Railway nearly half a million pounds and left a route not well designed for locomotive working. Despite this disaster, Brunel remained engineer to all the companies that built and operated sections of the Paddington-Penzance route, and many of his greatest works still lay ahead. Supreme was the Royal Albert Bridge at Saltash, opened in 1859, part suspension, part conventional bridge, the outward thrust of the two great tubes resting on the main spans balancing the inward thrust of the chains. Brunel was not at the opening but though in bad health he did live long enough to drive a trial train over it and beyond some miles into Cornwall. Another of those unkillable local legends, still solemnly taught in certain schools, is that he committed suicide from the bridge!

The bridge was indeed a magnificent success. The raising of each of its two gigantic central trusses were events that brought crowds from miles around, inspired poets and pamphleteers. I include a photograph of the bridge being built in the late 1850s.

Yet it is probably true to say that the broad gauge was another of Brunel's mistakes. In itself it was splendid: it had grace and stability, and made economic sense. The stability was proved in accidents, such as the first of the pair already mentioned at Norton Fitzwarren when an express plunged into a shunted goods train and sustained much less damage than a narrow-gauge train, with its greater overhanging of the track, would have suffered. But it should have been realised Britain was too small a country to support rival gauges, that the narrow or standard gauge had already become firmly established before Brunel entered the scene, and that indeed only with through trains would Burton-on-Trent beer reach the South West cheaply. Beer prices fell when the narrow gauge London & South Western reached Plymouth in the late 1870s; it shows how moribund the broad gauge had become that Plymouth actually gave its second railway a more hearty welcome than the first. So when the gauge was changed between Exeter and Truro that weekend in May 1892, to make a continuous narrow way from Paddington to Penzance, and allow through trains from the industrial north to Torbay and Cornish resorts, there were mixed feelings: sadness for the disappearance of the unique — and comfortable — institution, welcome for the new trade that standardisation would bring. Again poets and pamphleteers mingled with the crowds. Only a year before the railway had been continually in the headlines when the Great Blizzard caught many trains in snowdrifts, even in furthest Cornwall.

Paddington. It is here you test the legend that was the Great Western Railway. Be unmoved by this picture and for you the Great Way West is just a transport line only to be used to get you to your destination! But first look at the detail of this Royal occasion under Brunel's magnificent roof as passengers join specials for the royal garden party at Windsor in 1908. Paddington has a long association with royalty. Queen Victoria made her first train journey to the temporary station in 1842; several monarchs including King George VI had their body borne from the capital by funeral train.

The Route

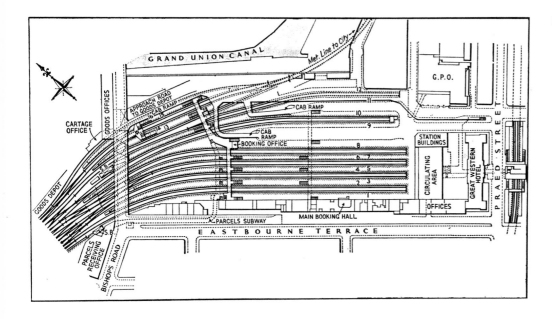

Paddington Station in 1954

Paddington to Penzance is a route of contrasts, and some of these go back to the history of the building of the railway by many different companies for different purposes.

PADDINGTON

Paddington station could be said to be the only building (as opposed to bridge and viaduct) of real architectural merit in the whole route to Penzance *via* Castle Cary. But many would place it first among London's termini. It is historic, spacious, functionally and architecturally satisfying. The second station, replacing a provisional terminus of 1838 slightly to the north west, it was opened in 1854, the first part on 16 January. The adjoining hotel, at the end of the mighty train shed, now the Great Western Royal Hotel, designed by Philip Hardwick, was opened the same year. The station lies in a cutting, and even those who love its interior have little idea what it looks like in its restricted landscape. But the interior quickly became famous; the graceful lines of Brunel's roof figure in W. P. Frith's famous painting, *The Railway Station*, showing people of all walks of life and all sorts of baggage joining a train. The painting, ten feet long, attracted over 21,000 people at a shilling a time during the first seven weeks it was on show in 1862. Paddington in fact was the first British station to have a large roof in metal; it was inspired by Paxton's Crystal Palace (Brunel had served on the Building Committee) and was beautifully executed with metal work by Sir Matthew Digby Wyatt including patterns contrived from Moorish motifs and metal tracery anticipating *art nouveau*. Many have been the changes to tracks and other arrangements, but the main train shed is timeless. No longer do 0-6-0 Pannier tanks, once such a feature of Paddington, puff in with empty trains — many trains are indeed now turned around and cleaned without ever leaving the station — but there is order and space here lacking at most other termini. The band still plays on the Lawn (the circulating area beyond the buffer stops) on weekend evenings.

PADDINGTON – READING

As far as Reading the train uses the original, superbly-built Great Western, authorised in 1835 and opened in stages between Paddington and Bristol between 1838 and 1841. Earthworks and bridges are hardly touched since Brunel's day. This is the best and certainly the most level of all exits from London, successions of trains taking a bare half hour, start to stop, for the 36 miles to Reading.

Paddington to Reading is of course quadruple track throughout. It is not the most scenic section, though the Thames is crossed over an original Brunel viaduct, the source of much controversy at the time of its building because of the very slight curve in the arches, at Maidenhead — and there is also a good view of the river as the train emerges from Sonning Cutting just short of Reading. Paddington is a superb terminus, functional and aesthetic; Reading, whose traffic has increased both with local population and the Heathrow Airport link, has long deserved better.

READING – WESTBURY

Immediately beyond Reading the line changes dramatically as the train veers sharply on to the Berks & Hants, at first built only as a local line and still subject to many irritating speed restrictions. It gradually climbs the broad open valley of the river Kennet and for many miles runs beside the delightful, moorhen-haunted Kennet & Avon canal, now being restored for pleasure traffic, to a summit at Savernake (note the canal tunnel). It then falls through the Vale of Pewsey and down the Stert Valley or Vale of the White Horse to Westbury (see map for views of white horses). The original Berks & Hants ran through Devizes, the section down the Stert Valley from Patney & Churton being of later origin (1900) and made for higher speed.

WESTBURY – CASTLE CARY

Here the train uses what was originally built as the Great Western's Weymouth branch, leaving the Paddington-Bristol line at Thingley Junction near Chippenham. Mileage posts west of Westbury still reflect the original route. The Westbury and Frome avoiding lines were additions of the 1930s. There is a steady climb to a summit at Brewham near Bruton.

CASTLE CARY – TAUNTON

From Castle Cary to Curry Rivel Junction and again from Athelney Junction to Cogload Junction the railway was newly built in the early years of this century for the 1906 opening of the shorter 'Via Castle Cary' route to the west; between Curry Rivel Junction and Athelney Junction the train follows the course of the Bristol & Exeter's Yeovil branch which was rebuilt at the same time. This is one of the more fascinating parts of the route, with lovely valleys before Somerton and the willow-growing area of Sedgemoor almost at sea level, and a glimpse of the Isle of Athelney before Taunton.

TAUNTON – EXETER

Trains via Castle Cary rejoin the original Great Way Round to the West at Cogload Junction, a few miles short of Taunton, and then follow the Bristol & Exeter Railway's main line to Exeter St David's. The Bristol & Exeter was almost as superbly built as the Great Western itself, though the ascent of Wellington Bank to Whiteball Tunnel spanning the Somerset/Devon border, and curves in the Cullompton district, prevent the 90mph running common on the rest of the route.

Handbills such as this were published almost daily dealing with local, excursion and express services. Here is a reminder that once stations such as Wellington had their regular clientele.

EXETER – PLYMOUTH

The line between Exeter and Plymouth was built by the South Devon Railway with headquarters at Exeter St Thomas, whose facade is still worth seeing although in semi-ruinous condition. Lacking the funds of the Great Western and the Bristol & Exeter, and having to contend with fiercer terrain, the South Devon was never so prosperous though always picturesque. Continuous high-speed running ends at Powderham where the railway first reaches salt water. It then hugs the Exe estuary to Dawlish Warren, runs between the red cliffs and sea from there to Teignmouth and beside the Teign estuary to Newton Abbot. Never miss this section! Climbing Dartmoor's foothills begins immediately after Newton Abbot, with a summit at Dainton, back to sea level at Totnes and a second summit at Wrangaton. Most of the climbing is consolidated into four main 'banks', two facing each way, Brunel planning to apply atmospheric power more thickly (by means of a larger pipe) on these sections than elsewhere. Atmospheric trains of course never travelled beyond Newton Abbot and so for 130 years steam and diesel locomotives have had to contend with gradients steeper than they need have been.

PLYMOUTH

The first station was a temporary terminus at Laira, where the locomotive depot is, but the original permanent station was Millbay near the docks, and trains for Cornwall went into the terminus and reversed. North Road, the present station, was a later addition, as was Cornwall Loop bypassing the now abandoned Millbay.

PLYMOUTH – TRURO

If the South Devon line had to be built on the cheap, most of it originally single track, the Cornwall Railway was a real economy exercise. Once over the magnificent Royal Albert Bridge at Saltash (you get a good view as the train turns almost 180 degrees after Saltash) the line twisted and turned on the up-and-over principle as it tried to avoid natural obstacles. So here you become much more intimate with the landscape, even though the original course has been abandoned at many parts by later improvements. The Cornwall Railway was a joint venture between the Great Western and the Bristol & Exeter and South Devon companies and was absorbed into the GW with the others in 1876.

TRURO – PENZANCE

Long before it was clear that a continuous track from London to the far west would ever materialise, mineral-rich Cornwall was busy developing its own railways, one of which, the Hayle Railway, was opened in 1837. The Hayle Railway ran from a low-level terminus in Hayle to Truro Newnham. It was later taken over by the West Cornwall Railway which rebuilt Penwithers Junction to give a link into the present Truro station, and diverted the route at the other end through the present high-level station in Hayle and so on to Penzance. The Hayle and West Cornwall Railways were built to standard gauge and not until 1866 was a third rail added to provide a 7ft way into Penzance, which lasted a mere twenty-six years before the final abolition of broad gauge. Many of Cornwall's historic mines as well as Hayle Harbour and Copperhouse Creek, handmaiden to Cornwall's industrial revolution, can be seen from the train; so can Mount's Bay over to Newlyn, St Michael's Mount and the intensive horticulture of west Cornwall, shortly before the train runs into Penzance station, still retaining its ugly wooden roof.

Seasons and Moods

The railway from Paddington to Penzance is a living thing, the same basic character but always changing its appearance in minor ways, with many distinct moods.

Throughout its history it has been mainly concerned with the carriage of passengers rather than goods. Indeed, mineral traffic and heavy freight have been conspicuous through their absence, and the route does not even figure on the modern freightliner map, a freightliner from London to Plymouth and St Blazey being withdrawn after an experimental period.

Dismissing freight traffic at this point, there has often been heavy mineral traffic within Cornwall itself, but nearly all of it has travelled only to Cornish ports or Plymouth, though in recent years more clay has been sent by rail to the Potteries, while a great roadstone quarry at Merehead on the former Witham to Yatton branch in Somerset now provides over twenty trains daily, and stone wagons can be seen occupying every available siding in the Westbury district. Produce of the land and sea have often figured more prominently, and for several generations one of the line's busiest periods was the broccoli season, when up to thirty trains a day (many composed of cattle wagons packed with broccoli to the roof) ran from various destinations in West Cornwall. On such occasions keeping the express passengers on time and finding enough empty wagons for the remainder of the crop were equally difficult. Daffodil time in the Scillies, strawberry time in the Tamar Valley, big fish harvests at Newlyn, Looe, Mevagissey and Brixham, and willow and teasel harvests in Somerset, added their touch of variety. The milk trains have been more regular, though even they run to something of a seasonal pattern, more milk being sent from Devon and Cornwall to the Home Counties at times of scarcity, in winter, and less at times of plenty when the London area satisfies more of its own demand and the West Country's surplus is turned into butter and cheese — and cream for local consumption at the height of the holiday season.

The route has always been a seasonal one, and throughout its length was developed and equipped for peak holiday passenger traffic, especially on summer Saturdays. It was in the mid 1920s that a separate summer-Saturday timetable was first printed, and in the 1930s and again for twenty years after the war at least three times the normal number of expresses ran on summer Saturdays, every locomotive, carriage, siding, signal box and railwayman being pressed into service.

Summer Saturdays in the West have made a separate book. Briefly, a summer Friday brought a general air of expectancy as machines and men got ready for the rush the following morning; the great invasion West began in the early hours of Saturday morning, thousands of passengers being disgorged at resorts like Torquay, Paignton and Newquay before breakfast. Many of the incoming trains were immediately reversed to begin the return rush, which traditionally had to be fitted into fewer hours with more critical timetabling. Since the railways continued to believe they had a social role as common carrier well into the motor age, they unprofitably handled a disproportionately high part of the extra peak traffic, especially at the beginning and end of the peak fortnight (the last week of July and first of August), during which some Devon and Cornwall resorts in fact received no less than one-third of their annual intake of visitors. The railwaymen's valiant work to provide extra seats and extra trains, to drag in old rolling stock and slower goods locomotives reducing the average speeds of all trains, in practice tended to hold back the move towards staggered holidays, which only fully came into its own when motorists refused to countenance delays of three hours on the Exeter bypass. One of the tragedies of the Paddington to Penzance service was that while it was excellent on Mondays to Fridays, many people first experienced it on a Saturday and suffered overcrowding, dirt and frustration. The usual tale even on the busiest summer Saturday was that Taunton was reached smartly; then troubles began. West of Taunton the double track had to accommodate the Bristol, Midlands and North traffic as well as that from Paddington, and only a few miles west of where the routes converge comes the steep rise of Wellington Bank, slowing the heartiest steam locomotive and necessitating banking with the heaviest passenger and goods trains.

When the line was at its most congested, trains could be stopped by signal as many as twenty-five times between Taunton and Newton Abbot, where the Torbay and Plymouth and Cornwall routes separate. Paignton, on the Torbay line, was a particular bottleneck, and trains queuing to be stowed in the sidings there sometimes stretched back on to the main line at Dawlish Warren, thus gratuitously delaying Cornish-bound services. Not that the pace of Cornish trains was all that quicker after Newton Abbot; most trains were made up to the maximum of fifteen coaches, had to stop at Newton Abbot to pick up a banking locomotive, and were stopped inordinately at Plymouth to change locomotives and maybe lose the restaurant car. The journey through Cornwall was then often at a snail's pace because of a poor power/weight ratio. Thus on the busiest days it was by no means exceptional for a train to take twice as long en route as on Monday to Friday. On Saturday afternoons there was another distinctive atmosphere as railwaymen began to sort out the accumulated muddle and empty trains had to be sent as far away as Bristol to find spare stabling. Such was the importance of the railway's service in the weekend change of visitors that local newspapers reported on the performance with as much interest as sports commentaries — and whether trains ran punctually and how many visitors they brought directly affected thousands of taxi proprietors, hoteliers and boarding house keepers, shop and other staff.

Christmas and Easter of course brought their minor rushes, many extra trains being run from Paddington before the holiday and returning after. But for years the railway was slow to provide adequate services for Londoners wishing to go to the South West for a weekend. Indeed, Paddington thought more in terms of day trips than weekend ones. In the 1920s, for instance, thousands of people from the London area paid day trips to places as far away as Newquay, infinitely further than they would plan to travel in their own car today. Yet in the 1950s often no extra train was provided for the growing number of weekenders leaving on Friday. Indeed, in the 1950s and early 1960s railway officials failed to grasp the fact that long-distance traffic potential was rising sharply as more Londoners retired to the sea and would use trains if they needed to go back to Town for business. At best, trains ran at two-hourly intervals, many stations suffering longer gaps. Apart from the *Cornish Riviera* and *Torbay Express*, all daytime services conveyed portions for both Plymouth and Torbay, which meant lengthy stops at Newton Abbot (or sometimes Exeter) for attaching and detaching. Only in recent times has the service been increased to a train an hour throughout the day as far as Newton Abbot, trains then going roughly alternately to Torbay and Plymouth. Only in the last ten years has there been an express at something like the best speed of the day to take West Country businessmen to London in the morning and bring them back in the evening: the *Golden Hind* is now one of the West Country's most important institutions, far more popular the year round than the *Cornish Riviera* itself, though the latter's 5½ hours for the 305 miles to Penzance is the line's all-time fastest.

The weather induced other moods. Perhaps one's vividest memories are inevitably of bright mornings after rainy nights. In showery weather the mood on the foothills of Dartmoor, or through the Cornish valleys, can change within seconds. Regular travellers watch the mood of the sea, which in rough weather intrudes itself, breaking over the train, sometimes washing away the ballast and closing one or both of the tracks between Teignmouth and Dawlish. Before its closure in 1958 the Teign Valley line would not infrequently be pressed into service to carry expresses inland on such occasions. It was because of the unreliability of the sea route that in the 1930s the Great Western put up a scheme (with Government help to relieve unemployment) for a diversion through the back of Dawlish and Teignmouth. Happily for those of us who love our sea and our estuary birds, no more was done than buying the land and fencing it off before war broke out.

Mention of war is a reminder of the large proportion of seats then taken by matelots on many trains, notably the time-honoured 8.45am from Plymouth to various destinations in the North; of several waves of evacuation traffic, heavier even than that on the busiest summer Saturday, at the time of Munich (when incidentally I myself first made acquaintance with the line), on the outbreak of war and at the beginning of the V1 and then the V2 rocket attacks. Paddington Station had a direct hit, Exeter St David's was damaged and much of the route on either side of the line through Plymouth and Devonport was flattened.

Many of the route's moods result from excursion and cheap-fare traffic. In the early days, the Plymouth Cheap, taking over twelve hours on the road, and of course overtaken by better trains, carried many a worker and West Country lass to better jobs or downfall. Emigration specials out of Cornwall after the collapse of the copper boom in the 1870s saw the break-up of many families. More happily, temperance specials did a roaring trade on the West Cornwall, one giant procession of three engines and 79 trucks judiciously breaking down by a cider orchard which the passengers stripped. It gave birth to a song with a chorus of:

> Happy Camborne, happy Camborne,
> Where the railway is so near;
> And the engine shows how water
> Can accomplish more than beer.

From the earliest days trains carried hordes of Exeter folk to the sea at Dawlish and Teignmouth, and until the 1950s up to 8,000 passengers travelled on fine days from Exeter St Thomas to Dawlish Warren alone. Before World War II local passengers predominated everywhere, most sections of line having more stopping services than expresses from London: two-thirds of Plymouth passengers joined the push-and-pull rail motors for stations to Saltash. Expresses too carried their quota of local passengers, a down express from Paddington often having more returning shoppers and schoolchildren to pick up than long-distance passengers to set down. Every section of the line had its tradition of Sunday-school outings, football and other specials. In the late 1930s the whole of Camborne, Redruth, Truro and St Austell seemed to use a succession of cheap Saturday trains to visit Plymouth.

Today there are more expresses than ever before. Speeds edge upwards with realignments, such as at Castle Cary and Teignmouth. Yet inevitably one thinks of the moods of yesteryear, the excitement with which schoolboys jotted down locomotive names (and what lovely names many of them were), the sadness on four occasions when chocolate-and cream livery disappeared, of the Reading slip-coach that seemed as permanent a feature of life as the waves breaking against the sea wall, of the water troughs where engines replenished their tanks at speed to make the non-stop journey from Paddington to Plymouth possible; of the mail exchanges between the nightly Travelling Post Office from Paddington to Penzance (also the North mail from Bristol to Plymouth) and various lineside installations.

The lineside apparatus has gone, along with water towers and troughs, but the TPO from Paddington still regulates much of our lives in the South West. One of the two exclusively mail trains run in Britain, it serves with its web of rail and road connections not only the whole of the West Country but a substantial slice of Southern England and all of South Wales. Sorters are at work on the train long before departure at 10.10pm. For an extra fee you can post a letter in the box on the side of the train itself. And here is an oddity: post a letter in any ordinary letter box at Paddington at 10.00pm and it will remain there undisturbed till next morning. But post it on the train and it will be taken down to Bristol, transferred there to the up Travelling Post Office, arrive back in Paddington in the early hours and be delivered first post with as much regularity as in anything these days. Likewise a letter for Plymouth posted on the up train at Newton Abbot will make a trip to Bristol and back; in fact there is an extension of the train in the form of a late box outside Newton's station, so you do not have actually to wait for the train to be at the platform.

Not only the up and down West of England Travelling Post Offices but services to and from Birmingham and South Wales are in Bristol Temple Meads together, a nocturnal reminder of the days when all traffic to Devon and Cornwall went that way. As it happens, on the very day of writing this the TPO suffered one of its rare breakdowns and my office in common with those throughout the South West had no 'up-country' mail in the morning. Incidentally, one of the reasons why mail takes longer in the Christmas rush is that due to the volume sorting on the train is temporarily abandoned. Normally mail for Penzance is sorted into streets before arrival in the same way that West Cornwall wholesale newsagents get to work sorting daily papers on the train.

The timetabling of any railway is a complex business, but the conflicting pressures on the Great Way West are exceptional. Expresses are generally governed by conditions at Paddington and Reading: it is so important to use every available 'path' for the evening exodus of businessmen's trains from Paddington that the arrival of a Penzance express at Reading (cutting across the Paddington-Swindon track) has to coincide with the non-stop passage through the station of the down Golden Hind. In fact up and down West of England trains are timed to be at Reading together on the hour almost throughout the day. Many up and down trains are also at Westbury together, both trains having connections to and from the Weymouth and Trowbridge lines. At Taunton, the Paddington services have to be fitted in with those from the North and Midlands; many a sharp run has proved pointless through the late running of a Birmingham train blocking the way at Taunton. At Exeter sensible connections have to be made with the Salisbury and Barnstaple lines and fast trains running non stop to Newton Abbot or Plymouth give connections to Dawlish and Teignmouth.

West of Exeter (less than half the way to Penzance in terms of time) trains start carrying substantial local traffic and indeed would not be economic unless at least some of the seats vacated by London passengers were not retaken. Yet while some passengers want to travel back from work from Exeter to Dawlish, or from Newton Abbot to Plymouth, or from Saltash to Bodmin Road or Lostwithiel, others are on 250 or 300 mile journeys and are displeased (and maybe start going by road, at least to Exeter) if the pace is slowed by too many stops. Mercifully the main line directly serves most of Devon's and Cornwall's important towns; those on the railway or within a few miles' drive from the nearest station have indeed grown more quickly than places a long way off such as Ilfracombe and Bude. For again those retiring to the West, or businessmen taking their light industries out of the home counties, measure isolation in terms of how quickly they — and their children or other relatives who do not drive — can get back to 'civilisation'.

The conflict between fast timings for long-distance passengers and serving schoolchildren, commuters and shoppers has been going on for over a century, but faster express timings following dieselisation and track improvements and then a total recasting of the service so that Paddington-Penzance trains left at half past odd instead of even hours caused exceptional strains and lost the railways many local regular customers. 'We are not interested in local traffic,' a senior railwayman once said, but the point has already been made that unless there are substantial numbers of local journeyings within the South West, trains become steadily emptier and less profitable as they go West — and anyway what is a 'local' journey? Newton Abbot to Redruth may not strictly be inter-city business but it is far longer that the total journey of many exclusively inter-city services.

That expresses really are faster is demonstrated by the number of Cornish people now taking day trips to London, without resorting to sleeper in either direction. The sleeping-car-only train remains another West Country institution, right down to the court case alleging rape (there was no segregation of sexes on the GWR third class sleepers; you merely drew a curtain to hide yourself in the compartment of four berths), but today the Truro businessman can spend the night at home and still be in London by 11.00am. But for prime ministers and ornithologists, the sleeper is the traditional way to the Scilly Isles.

Air services between London and Devon and Cornwall have been greeted enthusiastically on many occasions but usually wither away; there is no immediate prospect of a direct motorway; ironically drivers wanting to keep to dual track roads have to go the Great Way Round by Bristol and Bridgwater. So a greater proportion of people resort to the train than perhaps on any other route in Britain, and traffic continues to grow steadily reflecting the increase in the West Country's population and prosperity which the railway itself has sponsored.

There is a story behind every mile of track. Just before reaching Castle Cary the train from Paddington passes the deserted trackbed of the former Somerset & Dorset Railway at right angles. Just to the west, on the northern side, may be seen an embankment built at the demand of a court to link the two railways — built but never used. Further back toward London, at Savernake, one can trace the deserted trackbeds of two routes to Marlborough. These belonged to another cross-country line, the Midland & South Western Junction, from Cheltenham to Andover. The second line was built to avoid the Great Western's Savernake station because the bloody-minded GW persistently delayed the smaller company's trains — as it persistently stopped all London & South Western trains (including Plymouth ocean specials) at Exeter St David's. To take another example at random, at Liskeard in Cornwall the Looe trains start from a small terminus at right angles to the main station and then descend a steep loop to reach Combe Junction almost under Moorswater Viaduct carrying the main line high above the valley. There the branch trains join the old line running from mines down to Looe; the loop up to the main line station was a much later addition.

Along the track are the sites of several dozen deserted signalboxes, once the pride not only of the signalmen but of their locality. No longer do banking engines whistle their readiness to start assisting goods trains up inclines, for today all trains are kept within the weight limit of a single locomotive, even between Newton Abbot and Plymouth. The marshalling yeards at Hackney near Newton Abbot and Tavistock Junction near Plymouth are partly closed, today's marshalling point for much-reduced total traffic being Exeter Riverside. Engine sheds, where they exist at all, lack their old animation. One will never again hear the music of a King piloted by a Castle starting a fifteen-coach train out of Totnes up Rattery Bank. Even station announcements have lost some of their interest as through coaches no longer run down branch lines and generally fewer places are served. I used especially to enjoy hearing the departure of the 1.30pm from Paddington to Penzance with its ramifications all over the West. But let it be said British Railways still employ announcers with good Devon voices, especially at Exeter St David's. And one still wakes in the night to tell the time by the passage of trains including the *Owl*, so nicknamed through three generations. But as already said, the Travelling Post Office still brings our daily post, the newspaper train our reading matter, and rumours of stopping the line at Plymouth have been duly squashed. It is a railway still to be proud of, still to be enjoyed. As the *Cornish Riviera Limited* thunders under my office as I return from lunch I hope the passengers may have looked out of the window at the best points, will look back over Newton racecourse to Haytor and Dartmoor and will enjoy their run by the sea, will notice restoration work on the Kennet & Avon Canal and the picturesque waterside hamlets, and after a punctual arrival at Paddington following a steady 90 miles an hour plus on the final section from Reading will glance up at Brunel's magnificent roof before disappearing by taxi or underground.

Paddington. Two pictures of bustle and excitement at platform one. The opposite picture shows the *Cornish Riviera Express* ten minutes before departure in 1927; note the slip coach for Exeter at the rear, the main train running non-stop to Plymouth. The picture below was taken in 1904 and shows a West of England express then still routed by Bristol since the direct '*Via* Castle Cary' route to Devon and Cornwall was not opened until 1906.

Waiting for the road. Top, 2-2-2 No 3028 pilots another broad gauge locomotive on an unknown train around 1890. Left, tears come to the eyes of onlookers as an era ends. The time just before 10.15am on 20 May 1892, the train the *Cornishman* for Penzance, the last broad gauge train to leave Paddington. Opposite, top, *King Richard II* No 6021 waits on an empty train in February 1939, but the date could equally be ten or twenty years later. Bottom, *Western Duchess* leaves on a West Country train in May 1974. No longer are top West of England trains given the honour of platform one; indeed gone is the time-honoured ritual of a shunting engine (usually a pannier tank) bringing in the empty stock of arriving services, for today many trains are cleaned at the platform and maybe begin the return journey to Penzance 50 minutes after arrival.

Sonning Cutting contrasts. For over 100 years shutters have clicked a kaleidoscope of trains passing through Sonning Cutting, just east of Reading, and on almost any fine day since the line was opened in the 1830s enthusiasts, train spotters, or those more-casually interested have congregated on the bridges and embankments. Right, on the last day of the broad gauge in May 1892. Below, *Chepstow Castle*, No 4077, on an up Plymouth boat express, almost certainly carrying immigrants from the West Indies, in May 1955. Opposite, top, a more humble duty for Mogul No 6369 on a down goods in August 1960. In daylight hours probably less than five per cent of trains passing through the cutting are freights. Below, the Great Western's experimental gas turbine locomotive No 18000 with a Cheltenham express in 1955. Continuing its policy of individualism, the Great Western at one time believed steam power could be replaced by gas turbine while the other main companies were thinking of diesel.

The majesty of the broad gauge. Top left, a 4-2-2 heads the down *Zulu* express to the West near Ealing in 1890. Narrow gauge trains already predominate, the relief lines being exclusively narrow and the main lines mixed gauge. Bottom left, a 2-2-2 on a special in connection with Queen Victoria's Diamond Jubilee passes Acton. Below, a Twyford railwayman turns to get his face recorded by the camera rather than look at the approaching express to the West — one of the last to run, on 14 May 1892.

The first corridor train. The Great Western had many
virtues but the comfort of its passenger vehicles was
not one of them. Though much publicised, this
'vestibuled' train of about 1905 had third class
seating that would seem very spartan by today's
standards, novel though the open layout and the
tables then were. At first the connections between
coaches were kept locked and only used by the
guard and ticket collector, but by the beginning of
the first world war restaurant cars had become
common on expresses and passengers were given the
freedom of the train.

Top, King passes Castle. The down train, headed by
King Edward III, No 6022, is a summer Saturday
Falmouth express; Castle class *Earl of Shaftesbury,*
No 5062, is on a Swansea-Paddington express. The
date July 1960. Bottom, *Runter Hall,* No 7919,
crosses the Thames near Maidenhead by Brunel's
famous viaduct of flat arches with the 7.48am
through train from Henley-on-Thames to Paddington
in March 1963.

Top, bird's eye view of Reading in July 1973 with a
down express approaching the main down platform,
No 4, and an up express waiting to depart opposite.
The car park is partly on the site of the former
separate Southern terminus; a four-car multiple unit
train may be seen at the platform built to accommodate Southern Region trains. A second platform for
their use is being added at the time of writing. Also
in the picture may be seen Reading goods station
with the Thames beyond, and on the opposite side
of the track in the distance Reading gas works, one
of the unhandsome monuments of the route.
Bottom, *King Henry III,* No 6025, has pulled off the
main Paddington-Bristol route and passes through
Reading West at the beginning of the less busy Berks
& Hants section.

2-8-0s at Newbury. Top, a reminder that things did not always go smoothly in steam days, *The Royal Duchy* from Paddington to Penzance is in the hands of freight class 4700 in August 1958. It is seen passing Enborne Junction for the former cross-country route to Winchester and Southampton. Bottom, No 3844 of the more prolific 2800 class introduced as long ago as 1903 leaves Newbury with an empty stone train in July 1965.

Through Newbury. The down *Cornish Riviera Express* headed by No 6010 *King Charles I* on 7 June 1954. Note the 0-6-0 tender goods in the Lambourn Valley bay. It is only in recent years that a proportion of West of England expresses via Castle Cary have started calling at Newbury, now of course no longer a junction.

Kennet & Avon. For many miles the railway passes alongside the Kennet & Avon Canal, once an important highway from London to Bristol, later bought by the GWR and closed. It is now steadily being restored for pleasure traffic. Both these pictures are taken near Crofton. The top photograph shows a typically derelict pair of lock gates in 1970 with *Western Patriarch* heading a Paddington to Penzance train. The lower photograph shows *Western Queen* working a Penzance-Paddington train near the canal's Crofton pumping station in 1973. The canal will long outlive the Western class and other diesel hydraulic locomotives!

Westbury. The direct 'Via Castle Cary' route to the West lacks a single major town or traffic point all the way from the divergence from the original Great Way Round at Reading till it regains it at Taunton. But Westbury is a minor railway crossroads, some Paddington-West trains connecting with services via Trowbridge to Bath, to Salisbury and to Yeovil and Weymouth. Top, Derek Cross captures two Hymeks, Nos D7009 and D7037, on an empty train getting ready for Weymouth and on a Portsmouth-Bristol service, in August 1970. Bottom, once the *Torbay Express* was accorded almost as much importance and glory as the *Cornish Riviera*. Today the name is not used at all. By the time this picture was taken in April 1952, the train had been demoted to the extent of serving Westbury; it is seen taking the Westbury loop at Fairwood Junction.

Out in the country. Top, *King Henry VII*, No 6014, in experimental streamline casing, heads the down *Cornish Riviera* on the Frome bypass in September 1935. Bottom, King William IV, No 6002, on a West of England express also near Frome, in April the following year.

Local traffic. An auto-car train approaching Witham, junction for Shepton Mallet, Cheddar and Yatton, in 1935. Each section of line had a local service of sorts, but the service was often sparse and the numbers carried small. Local trains as well as expresses started using the 'cut off' between Castle Cary and Taunton in 1906, for instance, but it was too late in railway history to establish substantial new local traffic flows; staff often outnumbered passengers at those lovely-sounding places like Keinton Mandeville and Charlton Mackrell.

Taunton. Top, an up North of England train at Cogload Junction east of Taunton where the two routes from Paddington to the west converge. The fly-over junction, which allows trains from Bristol to cross the tracks *via* Castle Cary without interrupting traffic, and the quadrupling of the route from here through Taunton to Norton Fitzwarren, were improvements of the early 1930s. Bottom, but Taunton station itself had a major rebuild in 1895 when this photograph was taken of part of the workforce.

Left, among the Somerset hills. The up *Cornish Riviera Limited* crosses Somerset viaduct in September 1973.

Whiteball Tunnel. On a summer Saturday in 1958, No 5066 *Wardour Castle* races out of the tunnel with the 11.15 Plymouth-Paddington while No 6831 *Barley Grange* slogs up to the summit with the 10.20am Paddington-Kingswear, assisted by a banker from Wellington. Headcodes were provided on all summer Saturday trains to help signalmen identify them, but such was the density of traffic that mistakes were still made, such as a train due to stop at Exeter being signalled for the through non-platform track.

The old Exeter St David's. Top, an artist's impression (note the only partly drawn-in crossover in the left of the picture) of the arrival of the first train from Paddington, drawn by *Orion,* with driving wheels seven feet in diameter, on May Day 1844. The driver was Daniel Gooch, the locomotive superintendent of the Great Western, himself. He wrote: 'The whole time occupied in running the 388 miles to Exeter and back was 8 hours 29 minutes, or 45.7 miles per hour.' 130 years on and by a shorter route, it is still possible to experience journeys longer than the 4 hours and 21 minutes of his down trip and the 4 hours and 8 minutes of the return trip. Bottom, the interior of St David's in the 1920s before it lost its all-over roof.

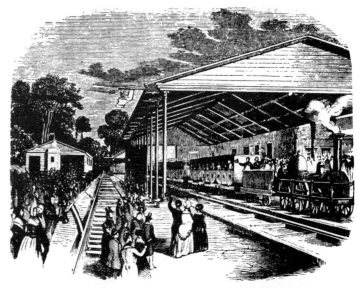

The joint station. Exeter St David's was perhaps the West Countrys most colourful station, that with the greatest number of historic happenings. This was partly due to its joint use by the London & South Western and later the Southern. As at Plymouth North Road, up Southern trains used down Western rails. The top picture on this page shows an Okehampton-Surbiton car carrier of 1962 at Cowley Bridge Junction joining the Western's down metals from Paddington. Below is a line up waiting departure at the West end of St David's with County class No 1000 *County of Middlesex* at platform one, 3Mt 2-6-2 tank No 82025 in the middle road, and *Battle of Britain* class No 34061 *73 Squadron* at platform three ready for the climb up to Exeter Central.

The picture opposite will evoke many memories, and for some readers the most nostalgic point will be the Southern banking loco-motive waiting its turn to help a train up the steep gradient to Exeter Central. Though Western trains predominated, the Southern called the tune with noise, notably whistling between banking and front engines of trains starting the climb. *King Henry III,* No 6025, has had to stop for water because Exminster troughs were out of action; nominally she is on a non-stop run from Plymouth-Paddington; a Castle is arriving on the 12.05pm Paddington-Plymouth on this summer Saturday in 1957.

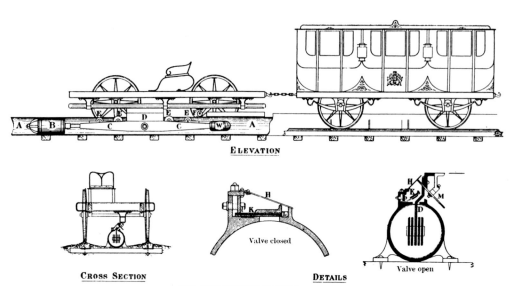

ELEVATION

CROSS SECTION

Valve closed

Valve open

DETAILS

THE ATMOSPHERIC SYSTEM

A.A. Continuous Pipe fixed between the rails.
B. Piston.
C.C. Iron Plates connected to the piston.
D. Plate connecting Apparatus to Carriage.

E. Metal Rollers to open the Continuous Valve.
F. Roller attached to Carriage for closing the Valve.
H. Weather Valve.[1]

K. Continuous Airtight Valve hinged at l.
L. Composition for sealing Valve.
M. Roller attached to Carriage for opening Weather Valve.[1]
W. Counterweight to Piston.

[1] These complications do not appear to have been in use on the South Devon Railway.

The railway between Exeter and Newton Abbot has probably been more illustrated per mile than any other line in the world. There are several reasons for this. There is outstanding river, sea and cliff scenery. The story of the railway itself is unusually fascinating: here broad gauge atmospheric trains were once delayed by the sea breaking over the track. The railway runs smack between the resort of Dawlish and its beaches, always inviting the attention of photographers, amateur and professional. Amateurs have included many railwaymen taking holidays in the district, some at the railway's own convalescent home in Dawlish; professionals include the Chapman family who ran a postcard and photographic business in Dawlish and whose son is incidentally now in charge of packing at David & Charles. So no excuse is made for devoting a disproportionate number of pages to this section. Left is a sketch of how the atmospheric system worked and below a picture of a section of pipe recovered after many years' use as a sewer outfall. Opposite is an example of the many different types of pictorial treatment accorded the railway in the days before cameras.

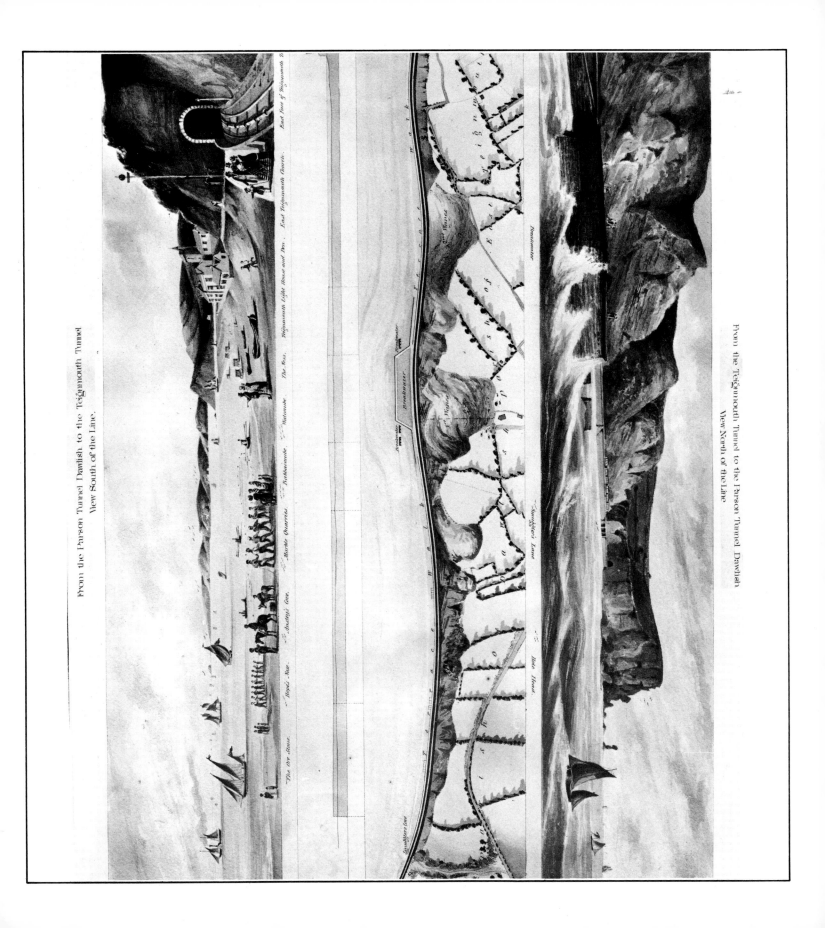

From the Parson Tunnel Dawlish to the Teignmouth Tunnel
View South of the Line.

From the Teignmouth Tunnel to the Parson Tunnel Dawlish
View North of the Line

Where atmospheric trains once gathered speed, on
the outskirts of Exeter near Countess Wear and the
Exeter bypass with a distant view of Exeter
Cathedral. Paddington-Plymouth express is hauled
by *Llandovery Castle*, No 5001. The land on either
side the track at this point has since been developed
for light industry.

Rough seas. Above, an artist's impression of the late 1840s from the *Illustrated London News*. Below, one of the Chapman photographs showing a salt-sprayed freight train passing through Dawlish. One wonders what damage was done to the cargo. This photograph was eagerly bought in postcard form by thousands of visitors enjoying finer weather. In 1974 there was further evidence of what the sea can do in winter: throughout the year most of Dawlish's down platform was missing having been destroyed in an exceptional gale.

ROUGH SEA, DAWLISH   28447

THE EXE ESTUARY. COCKWOOD. 25549

A double spread of Chapman photographs that sold widely as postcards. Top, the train in its setting; note the two gas-carrying vehicles at the front of the train. They were once as common as cattle wagons. Middle, the beginning of Dawlish Warren, a small handful of passengers alighting from a steam railcar which ran between St Thomas and Teignmouth. Bottom left, by 1914 the track through the station had been quadrupled and several thousand passengers were arriving on fine Sundays and Bank Holidays. The building on the up platform is now a railway museum. Bottom right and opposite top are two views showing the railway beside the beach in different eras. Bottom opposite, visitors and residents of the 1900s pose following the crash of an up passenger train into a goods that had been shunted onto the up track to allow an express to pass; this would have been before the provision of the loop at Dawlish Warren.

The Warren Halt, Dawlish

G.W. RY. STATION. DAWLISH WARREN 13521

Dawlish. Just before the outbreak of war in 1939,
the up *Cornish Riviera,* mainly composed of
'Centenary' coaches whose end doors were inset
from the body work, turns inland near Langstone
Rock. Opposite, the down *Cornish Riviera* of May
1971, passes through Dawlish headed by a single
Warship though at that date the schedule demanded
two locomotives.

A run-of-the-mill train captured by an outstanding photographer, Derek Cross. No 6812, *Chesford Grange,* passes Dawlish Warren on a Kingswear-Swindon train in September 1959.

Removing a bottleneck. The section between Dawlish and Parson's Tunnel, through five short tunnels, was the last section of the Paddington-Plymouth route to be doubled, work starting in 1902 and not being finished till 1905. The top picture shows a train on the single track at the turn of the century: *Princess Louise*, No 3075, is on an up express. Below we see men at work in 1904, incidentally at the same time that an army of labourers — paid 6d (2½p) an hour — were completing the links in the *'Via* Castle Cary' route.

The picture we perhaps remember best; an express
emerging from the last of the five tunnels at the
Parson and Clerk rocks, much eroded even during
our lifetime, to run along the Sea Wall proper to
Teignmouth. Here the train is the *Torbay Express*
in an official British Railways photograph much
used for publicity purposes.

Teignmouth. Top, along the Sea Wall *County of Montgomery*, No 1021 of the last Great Western express locomotive design, heads a Paignton to Liverpool train in July 1955. Below, another rare shot of men at work, this time on the rebuidling of Teignmouth station in the 1890s. Opposite, the spot where many children first saw a Great Western train, at the Teignmouth end of the Sea Wall . The driver is typically waving to a group of unseen people watching his progress. The Castle is on a London-bound train in August 1956.

Newton Abbot has been an important junction for 130 years and for over a century had active locomotive and carriage building and repair shops. At one time over half the town's workforce was employed by the railways. The whole district's morning and lunch-time routines were governed by the steam hooter telling railwaymen to report for duty, while so close was the link between town and railway that when the Great Western opened a new station in 1927 the clocks were provided by public subscription. Newton Abbot has, however, also been a place of monumental delays. For generations the worst hold ups were to Torbay trains waiting for platform space — the middle platform used by them is shown in the picture of the old station on this page. Something of the atmosphere of this steam centre of the west is conveyed in the picture opposite, taken in 1953. Note the trucks of locomotive coal being shunted to the extreme right; the west dock to the extreme left is now abandoned, as also is the town's power station in the distance. The telephone wires and vapour trail add their own touch.

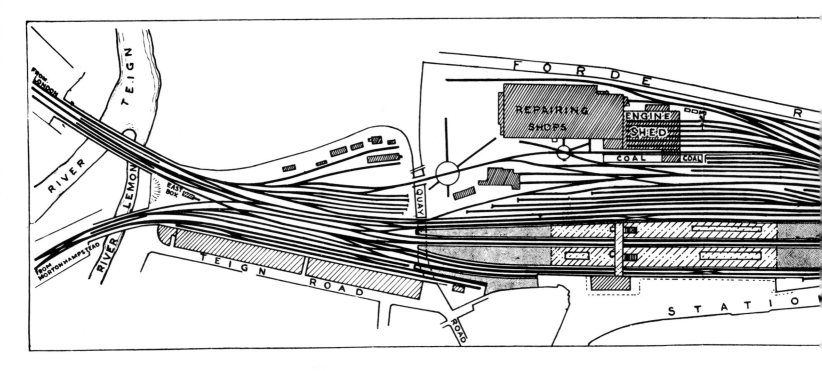

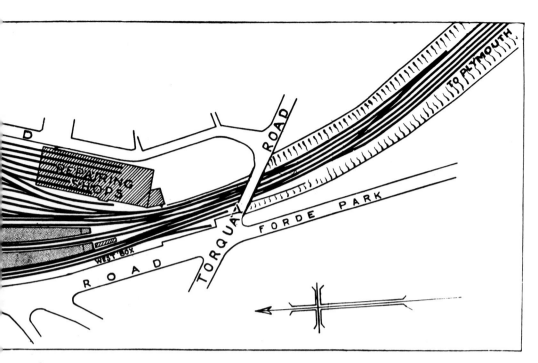

Newton Abbot. Left is the plan of the new layout as opened in 1927. Below right, a close-up of the signals mid-way down the centre platform we look out on from the offices of David & Charles, still GWR lower quadrant in 1975. All four main platform faces were originally given two numbers and signalled to take two trains, the tracks serving the outer faces having scissors crossovers to facilitate the attaching and detaching of Torbay portions. Below left, a shot of two trains leaving the west end of the old station still retaining an overall roof for Torbay and Plymouth respectively. To the extreme right can be seen the end of Railway Cottages and their gardens with three children watching the trains. These cottages received a direct hit during the war when a German bomber was aiming at a train heading for Plymouth. David & Charles have built offices on the site and also taken over the carriage and wagon repair shops seen next to it.

Left. Cars climbing Dainton Bank. The summer-only
Motorail includes a daily service from London
(Kensington Olympia) to St Austell. Below. A little
higher up the same bank, at Stoneycombe Quarry
(now providing several daily trains of ballast)
No 7814, *Fringford Manor*, pilots No 1017, *County
of Hereford* on a Penzance-Wolverhampton train in
August 1958.

West of Newton Abbot. The picture below shows
the Kingswear section of a London train arriving
behind 51XX, No 6166. The Kingswear/Torbay
section was normally scheduled to stand at Newton
Abbot 15 minutes, the Plymouth/Cornwall section
arriving afterwards, its locomotive being released
over a scissors crossover half way down the long
platform and running round the Kingswear coaches
in front. At the other end of the last piece of
quadruple track in the West, at Aller Junction,
opposite, a double-headed express approaches
from Plymouth while a Paignton train waits for
signals. On summer Saturdays most Paignton
trains stopped here and at other points because
of the bottleneck at Paignton itself — the queue
sometimes stretching back beyond Newton Abbot
and so delaying Plymouth and Cornwall trains.

On either side of Dainton. This page, Nos 4174 and 1008 near Stoneycombe Quarry with a return excursion from Paignton to Plymouth in 1958. Right, two Castles, Nos 5024 and 7032, with an up milk train approaching Dainton Tunnel the same year. At this moment the train could be heard for many miles around and local experts interpreted the way the sound carried to help foretell the weather.

Dainton Bank. A classic picture by Peter Gray near the end of the steam era, in summer 1961: No 4948 *Northwick Hall*, climbs vigorously in Dainton gorge half way up the incline from Newton Abbot to Dainton Tunnel.

Local activity at Totnes. 0-4-2 No 1470 with the Ashburton (later known as Dart Valley) line auto-train has just filled its tanks with water while standing on the up through track, while a West Country class locomotive of the Southern Region stands in the up platform on a main line stopping service. Southern locomotives and men worked two daily services each way between Exeter and Plymouth for many years to keep staff familiar with alternative routes between the two cities. To the right of the picture may be seen the Totnes harbour branch now closed and removed.

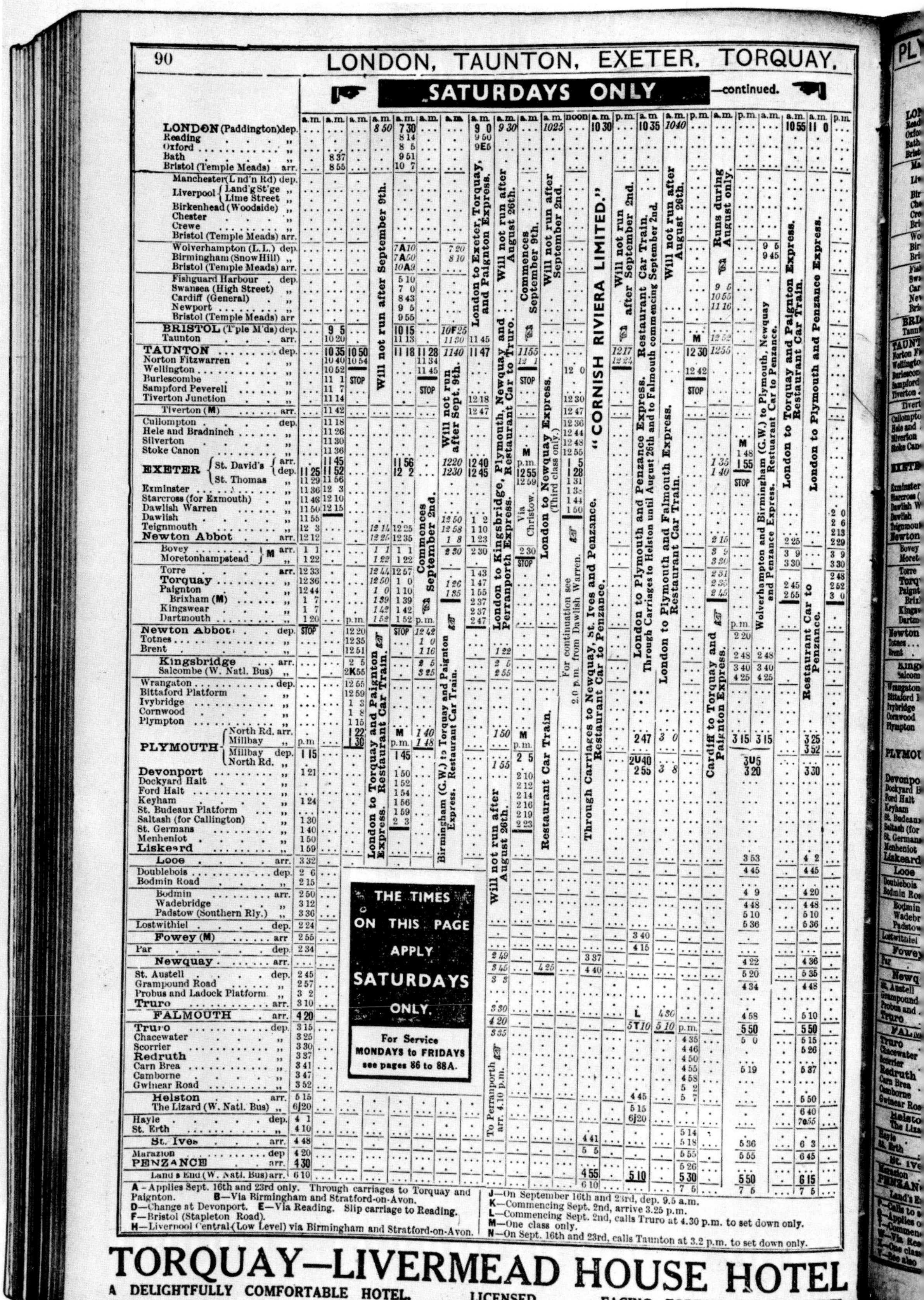

☞ SATURDAYS ONLY —continued. ☜

		a.m.	a.m.	a.m.	a.m.	a.m.	a.m.	a.m.	a.m.	noon	a.m.	p.m.	p.m.	p.m.	a.m.	a.m.	p.m.
LONDON (Paddington)	dep.			8 50	7 30		9 0	9 30		10 25		10 30	10 35	10 40		10 55	11 0
Reading	"				8 14		9 50										
Oxford	"				8 5		9 E5										
Bath	"		8 37		9 51												
Bristol (Temple Meads)	arr.		8 55		10 7												
Manchester (L'nd'n Rd)	dep.																
Liverpool { Land'g St'ge	"															9 6	
Lime Street	"															9 45	
Birkenhead (Woodside)	"																
Chester	"																
Crewe	"																
Bristol (Temple Meads)	arr.																
Wolverhampton (L.L.)	dep.				7 A10		7 20										
Birmingham (Snow Hill)	"				7 A50		8 10										
Bristol (Temple Meads)	arr.				10 A9												
Fishguard Harbour	dep.				5 10												
Swansea (High Street)	"				7 0											9 6	
Cardiff (General)	"				8 43											10 55	
Newport	"				9 5											11 16	
Bristol (Temple Meads)	arr.				9 55												
BRISTOL (T'ple M'ds)	dep.		9 5		10 15		10 F25										
Taunton	"		10 20		11 13		11 50	11 45									12 52
TAUNTON	dep.		10 35	10 50	11 18	11 28	11 40	11 47		11 55		12 17		12 30	12 55		
Norton Fitzwarren	"		10 40	10 54		11 34				12 1		12 24					
Wellington	"		10 52			11 45				12 0				12 42			
Burlescombe	"		11 1	STOP								STOP					
Sampford Peverell	"		11 7			STOP											
Tiverton Junction	"		11 14							12 30							
Tiverton (M)	arr.		11 42					12 18		12 47							
Cullompton	dep.		11 18					12 47		12 36							
Hele and Bradninch	"		11 26							12 47							
Silverton	"		11 30							12 55							
Stoke Canon	"		11 36							12 55							
EXETER { St. David's	arr.	11 25	11 45		11 56		12 20	12 40		12 55			1 28		1 35	1 48		
{ St. Thomas	dep.	11 25	11 52		12 2		12 30	12 45		12 59			1 31		1 40	1 55		
Exminster	"	11 29	11 56										1 32		STOP			
Starcross (for Exmouth)	"	11 36	12 3										1 32					
Dawlish Warren	"	11 48	12 10				12 50	1 2					1 44					
Dawlish	"	11 50	12 15				12 58	1 10					1 50					
Teignmouth	"	11 55					1 4	1 16										
Newton Abbot	arr.	12 3					1 10	1 23										
		12 12			12 14	12 25							2 15					
Bovey	"	1 1			12 25	12 35												
Moretonhampstead	arr.	1 22			1 22	1 22		2 30	2 30				3 9			3 9		
Torre	arr.	12 33			12 44	12 57							3 30			3 30		
Torquay	"	12 36			12 50	1 0		1 43					2 30		2 45	2 48		
Paignton	"	12 44			1 0	1 10		1 26	1 55				2 36		2 55	2 52		
Brixham (M)	arr.	1 7			1 39	1 39		1 55					2 40			3 0		
Kingswear	"	1 7			1 42	1 42		2 37										
Dartmouth	"	1 20			1 52	1 52		2 37										
Newton Abbot	dep.	STOP			12 20		STOP	12 42					2 20					
Totnes	"				12 35			1 0										
Brent	"				12 51			1 16										
Kingsbridge	arr.				2 5			2 5					2 48	2 48				
Salcombe (W. Natl. Bus)	"				2 K55			3 25					3 40	3 40				
Wrangaton	dep.				12 59			1 22					4 25	4 25				
Bittaford Platform	"				12 59													
Ivybridge	"				1 3			2 5										
Cornwood	"				1 9			2 55										
Plympton	"				1 15													
PLYMOUTH { North Rd. arr.					1 22			1 40			1 50		2 47	3 0		3 15	3 15	3 25
{ Millbay	arr.	p.m.			1 30			1 48		p.m.		M						3 52
{ Millbay	dep.	1 15						1 45			2 5		2 U40	3 5		3 U5		
{ North Rd.	dep.	1 15									2 55	3 8		3 20		3 20		3 30
Devonport		1 21						1 50										
Dockyard Halt	"							1 52										
Ford Halt	"							1 54			1 55							
Keyham	"	1 24						1 56										
St. Budeaux Platform	"							2 10										
Saltash (for Callington)	"	1 30						2 16			2 12							
St. Germans	"	1 40						2 19			2 16							
Menheniot	"	1 50						2 23			2 19							
Liskeard	"	1 59									2 23							
Looe	arr.	3 32													3 53		4 2	
Doublebois	dep.	2 6													4 45		4 45	
Bodmin Road	"	2 15																
Bodmin	arr.	2 50													4 9		4 20	
Wadebridge	"	3 12													4 48		4 48	
Padstow (Southern Rly.)	"	3 36													5 10		5 10	
Lostwithiel	dep.	2 24													5 36		5 36	
Fowey (M)	arr.	2 55									3 40							
Par	dep.	2 34																
Newquay	arr.							2 49		3 37					4 22		4 36	
St. Austell	dep.	2 45						3 45	4 25	4 40					5 20		5 35	
Grampound Road	"	2 57						3 3							4 34		4 48	
Probus and Ladock Platform	"	3 2																
Truro	arr.	3 10																
FALMOUTH	arr.	4 20						3 30							4 58		5 10	
Truro	dep.	3 15						4 20					L		5 50		5 50	
Chacewater	"	3 25						3 35					5 T10	5 10	5 0		5 15	
Scorrier	"	3 30													4 35		5 20	
Redruth	"	3 37													4 46			
Carn Brea	"	3 41													4 50		5 37	
Camborne	"	3 47													4 55			
Gwinear Road	"	3 52													4 58			
Helston	arr.	5 15										4 45			5 7		5 50	
The Lizard (W. Natl. Bus)	"	6 J20										5 15					6 40	
Hayle	dep.	4 1										6 J20			5 14		7 0 55	
St. Erth	"	4 10													5 18			
St. Ives	arr.	4 48									4 41				5 18	5 36		
Marazion	dep.	4 20									5 5				5 55	5 55		
PENZANCE	arr.	4 30																6 45
Land s End (W. Natl. Bus) arr.		6 10						4 55	5 10				5 30		5 50		6 15	

Vertical notes in columns (left to right):

- Will not run after September 9th.
- London to Exeter, Torquay, and Paignton Express.
- Will not run after August 26th.
- Commences September 9th.
- Will not run after September 2nd.
- Commences September 2nd.
- London to Kingsbridge, Plymouth, Newquay, and Perranporth Express. Restaurant Car to Truro.
- London to Newquay Express. (Third class only.)
- Via Christow.
- **"CORNISH RIVIERA LIMITED."** Will not run after September 2nd. Restaurant Car Train.
- London to Plymouth and Penzance Express. Through Carriages to Helston until August 26th and to Falmouth commencing September 2nd.
- London to Plymouth and Falmouth Express. Restaurant Car Train.
- Runs during August only.
- Cardiff to Torquay and Paignton Express.
- Wolverhampton and Birmingham (G.W.) to Plymouth, Newquay and Penzance Express. Restaurant Car to Penzance.
- London to Torquay and Paignton Express. Restaurant Car Train.
- London to Plymouth and Penzance Express.

THE TIMES ON THIS PAGE APPLY SATURDAYS ONLY.

For Service MONDAYS to FRIDAYS see pages 86 to 88A.

Footnotes:

A—Applies Sept. 16th and 23rd only. Through carriages to Torquay and Paignton.
B—Via Birmingham and Stratford-on-Avon.
D—Change at Devonport.
E—Via Reading. Slip carriage to Reading.
F—Bristol (Stapleton Road).
H—Liverpool Central (Low Level) via Birmingham and Stratford-on-Avon.
J—On September 16th and 23rd, dep. 9.5 a.m.
K—Commencing Sept. 2nd, arrive 3.25 p.m.
L—Commencing Sept. 2nd, calls Truro at 4.30 p.m. to set down only.
M—One class only.
N—On Sept. 16th and 23rd, calls Taunton at 3.2 p.m. to set down only.

To Perranporth arr. 4.10 p.m.

A page from the Great Western's summer timetable of 1939. Note the split destination of the *Cornish Riviera Limited*. Some extra Summer Saturday trains ran even in the darkest days of hostilities and after the war the timetable was again very similar, extra peak period trains being added to reach a maximum density in the early 1950s

On the Dartmoor foothills. Left, a Castle piloting a
King halted by signals on an up train outside Brent.
Above, the up *Cornish Riviera* passing Bittaford
Platform, *Goytrey Hall*, No 4929, piloting *King
Charles II*, No 6009. Both are pictures of the mid-
1950s. Shortly afterwards a diesel began piloting
the train whose main locomotive remained a King
for several further years.

Viaducts. Top, a broad gauge train at Ivybridge just before crossing the viaduct in its original single-track form. Doubling did not take place till after the abolition of the broad gauge in 1892. Bottom, an early lithograph of Slade Viaduct near Cornwood.

tor Train
Saltash Station

Plymouth suburban services. Once Plymouth had a massive suburban service, on the London & South Western as well as Great Western lines, halts and platforms supplementing ordinary stations. The busiest route was always that to Saltash, mainly because the alternative road and ferry journey was slow. The steam railcar shown in the top photograph was introduced around 1910 but was soon replaced by push-and-pull trains using separate locomotives but with driving controls repeated at the far end of the coach. Indeed, at busy times, morning and evening, a locomotive would be sandwiched between two auto-cars on either side of it, the ensemble carrying up to 500 passengers. The opening of the Saltash road bridge immediately cut traffic, but although they had withdrawn other suburban services by the early 1930s the railways were reluctant to abandon the Saltash route, and some extra trains purely for the local traffic survived into the 1960s. Below is shown the return of the last steam working to Plymouth at midnight in December 1959.

Left, Brunel's *pièce de résistance* at Saltash as seen through the driver's window of a multiple unit train. Cornishmen complained the bridge would let the devil in; it certainly let in national unifying influences and carried away many Cornishmen to live and work elsewhere. Nearly 120 years later it is used by far heavier trains (including 100-ton wagons) than were ever envisaged by Brunel, and despite the new road bridge alongside (which has something of a dwarfing effect) it remains vital to Cornwall's economy providing the quickest link with 'up country' for passengers, mail and newspapers, milk and much else.

The Royal Albert Bridge, Saltash. The top picture shows the bridge as seen by a passenger of a Penzance-bound train after it has turned an angle of almost 180 degrees while passing through Saltash. Especially when there used to be an intensive Plymouth-Saltash suburban service of rail motors, passengers could often see preceding or following trains, and an incident such as a swan refusing to budge from the track could cause big delays. Right is the Cuneo poster commissioned for the bridge's centenary in 1959. The bridge was floodlit that season, just before powers were obtained to build the road bridge to the north.

Left is one of the photographs taken in the early days of the camera during the construction of the Royal Albert Bridge. The first of the two main trusses has been raised into position and the second is being got ready.

End of the broad gauge. Throughout the route from Taunton to Truro, small gangs of men such as this drew in one rail to convert the gauge from broad to narrow in a single weekend in May 1892. 'Comfort has had to give way to convenience,' was the Press comment; convenience included the possibility of through trains and trucks from the Midlands and North of England. Soon, for instance, Burton-on-Trent beer was to increase in popularity in Cornwall, through vehicles making it more competitive with local beers. The act of conversion was however a sober affair conducted with ceremony but great seriousness and leaving a lasting impression on the minds of onlookers as well as those taking part. Both the picture and the certificate concern the Menheniot section.

GREAT WESTERN RAILWAY.

"CONVERSION OF GAUGE."

Menheniot This is to certify that the Line between and *Saltash* is ready to be re-opened for Traffic, and the ordinary working of Trains between those points can be resumed on Monday, the 23rd.

W. H. Wright, { *Traffic Inspector.*

To the Station Master *S. Germans* Station.

May 20th, 189?

Cornwall Railway viaducts. These two photographs date from the late 1890s and show Coldrennick Viaduct near Menheniot and old Liskeard Viaduct with Brunel's timberwork branching out from the top of the stone piers. Fire was the biggest hazard with timber viaducts and tanks of water were kept at each end of each viaduct.

8.00am Penzance-Plymouth diesel multiple-unit train entering Lostwithiel.

Par. Busy scene on 1 September 1972 as No 1065 *Western Consort* arrives on up *Cornishman* from Penzance to Leeds while the Newquay train which has brought most of the waiting passengers waits to return down the branch. The branch is double track just round the bend to St Blazey, and for many years an up train on the main line connected with down and up trains on the branch, the down one leaving and passing the up one while the express waited at the platform. St Blazey's locomotive depot serviced several main line trains as well as the Newquay branch and the china clay traffic. Par was one of several Cornish stations whose refreshment room was patronised by passing motorists and local people as well as by train travellers and railway staff. Another was at Bodmin Road.

Truro station shortly after rebuilding in the late 1890s. So much has changed yet so much remains the same that this is a particularly interesting photograph. For over 80 years since it was taken, trains for Falmouth have waited in the bay platform at the extreme right. With branch trains from Newquay via Perranporth (not at this date since the line had not yet been opened and hence no mention of it on the station nameplate) as well as Falmouth, and terminating local services from Plymouth and Penzance, Truro was once an extremely busy station, handling about 1,500 local passengers daily in addition to those making longer journeys. Note the sharp curve on to the viaduct at the end of the station: passengers have a grand view of the city and its Cathedral from the viaduct.

West Cornwall. The top picture shows the original terminus of the Hayle Railway with the foundry in the background and the connecting omnibus for Penzance. Middle, one of the famous lengthy West Cornwall temperance specials on the viaduct above Hayle by which the railway was carried forward as the West Cornwall Railway to Penzance. Bottom, two snapshots of broad gauge trains at Marazion and Redruth on the mixed gauge West Cornwall. Note the hand signal at Marazion.

Penzance. The last mile into Penzance runs beside the sea with fine views of Mounts Bay. Before sea defences were strengthened (and incidentally they required further strengthening in 1975) the weather created almost more interruptions here than along the sea wall between Dawlish and Teignmouth. Once the West Cornwall Railway had so many locomotives cut off at its terminus that it guided several by road around the interruption. The top picture shows how vulnerable the track remained years later, after the abolition of the broad gauge. It shows Duke class *Armorel*, No 3273, leaving on an up express. Below and opposite are two views in very different mood of the terminus with its wooden roof. The picture below shows the Mayor starting the first run of a new express on 1 July 1901; this was the precursor of the *Cornish Riviera Express* started three years later. The picture opposite shows a busy scene in the late 1960s.

Penzance. A final and nostalgic glimpse of the end of the line beside a harbour full of sailing craft probably around 1890 with mixed gauge track. The wooden roof remains just the same today (see previous page), but the railway has demanded more room for its operations. Penzance has actually shrunk in population since the picture was taken. Once it was a true metropolis of the far west, with a highly-developed cultural life and many other facilities not normally found outside major cities. It served a large area dependent on mining, fishing and sailing. The opening of through services from London in 1859 was timely for within a decade Cornish mining had passed its peak and the growth of horticulture made possible by fast rail transits helped combat the loss of work. At the height of the broccoli and flower seasons, the railway itself employed many extra hands and up to a hundred horse-drawn vehicles were said to be waiting to unload their produce one day at Marazion, the next station up the line.

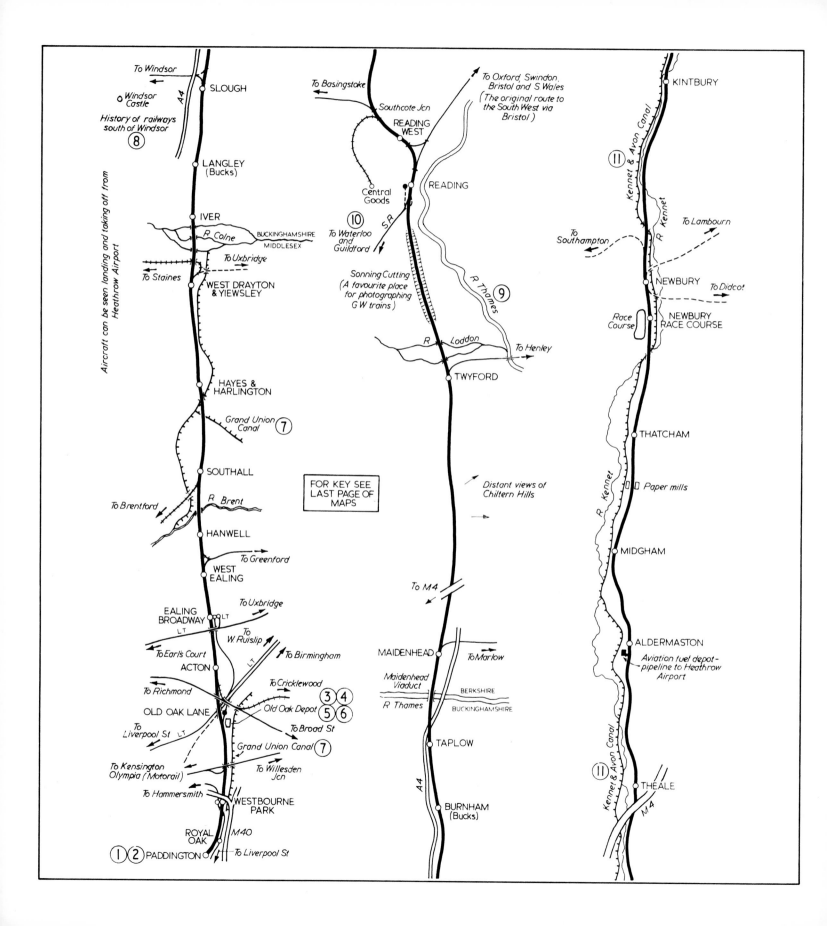

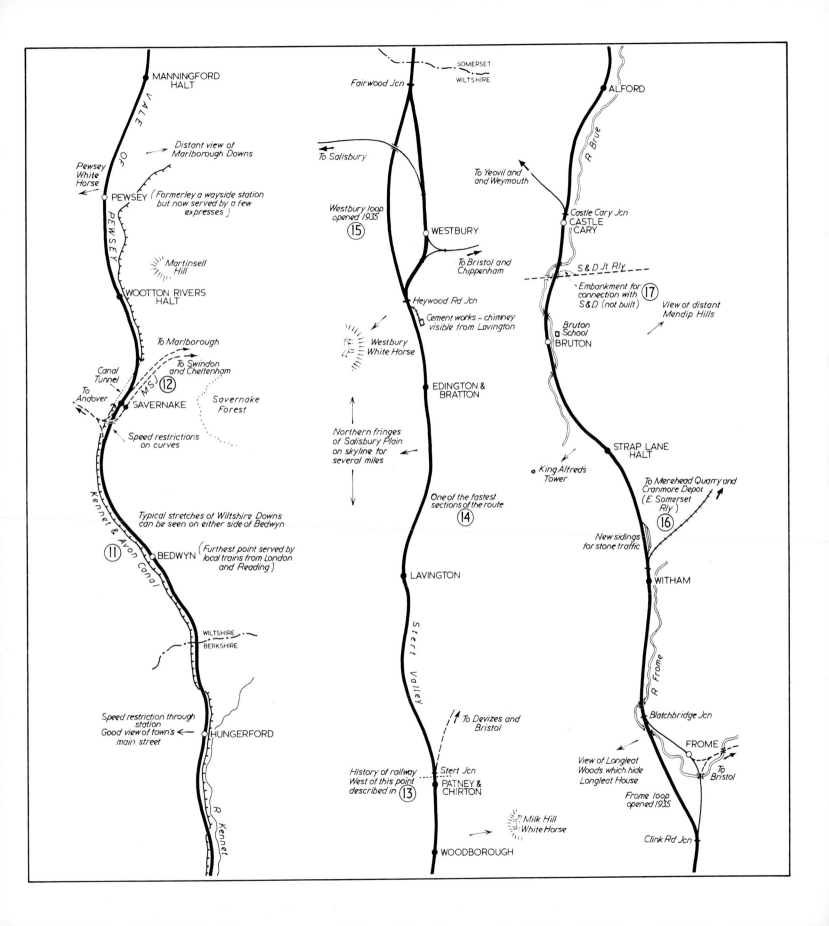

MANNINGFORD HALT

VALE

Distant view of Marlborough Downs

Pewsey White Horse

OF

PEWSEY *(Formerley a wayside station but now served by a few expresses)*

PEWSEY

Martinsell Hill

WOOTTON RIVERS HALT

To Marlborough

Canal Tunnel

To Swindon and Cheltenham

MSJ ⑫

To Andover

SAVERNAKE

Savernake Forest

Speed restrictions on curves

Typical stretches of Wiltshire Downs can be seen on either side of Bedwyn

Kennet & Avon Canal

⑪ BEDWYN *(Furthest point served by local trains from London and Reading)*

WILTSHIRE
BERKSHIRE

Speed restriction through station
Good view of town's main street HUNGERFORD

R. Kennet

Fairwood Jcn

SOMERSET
WILTSHIRE

To Salisbury

Westbury loop opened 1935 ⑮

WESTBURY

To Bristol and Chippenham

Heywood Rd Jcn

Cement works – chimney visible from Lavington

Westbury White Horse

EDINGTON & BRATTON

Northern fringes of Salisbury Plain on skyline for several miles

One of the fastest sections of the route ⑭

LAVINGTON

Stert Valley

To Devizes and Bristol

History of railway West of this point described in ⑬ Stert Jcn
PATNEY & CHIRTON

Milk Hill White Horse

WOODBOROUGH

ALFORD

R Brue

To Yeovil and and Weymouth

Castle Cary Jcn
CASTLE CARY

S & D Jt. Rly

Embankment for connection with S&D (not built) ⑰

View of distant Mendip Hills

Bruton School
BRUTON

STRAP LANE HALT

King Alfred's Tower

To Merehead Quarry and Cranmore Depot (E. Somerset Rly)

New sidings for stone traffic ⑯

WITHAM

R Frome

Blatchbridge Jcn

FROME

View of Longleat Woods which hide Longleat House

To Bristol

Frome loop opened 1935

Clink Rd Jcn

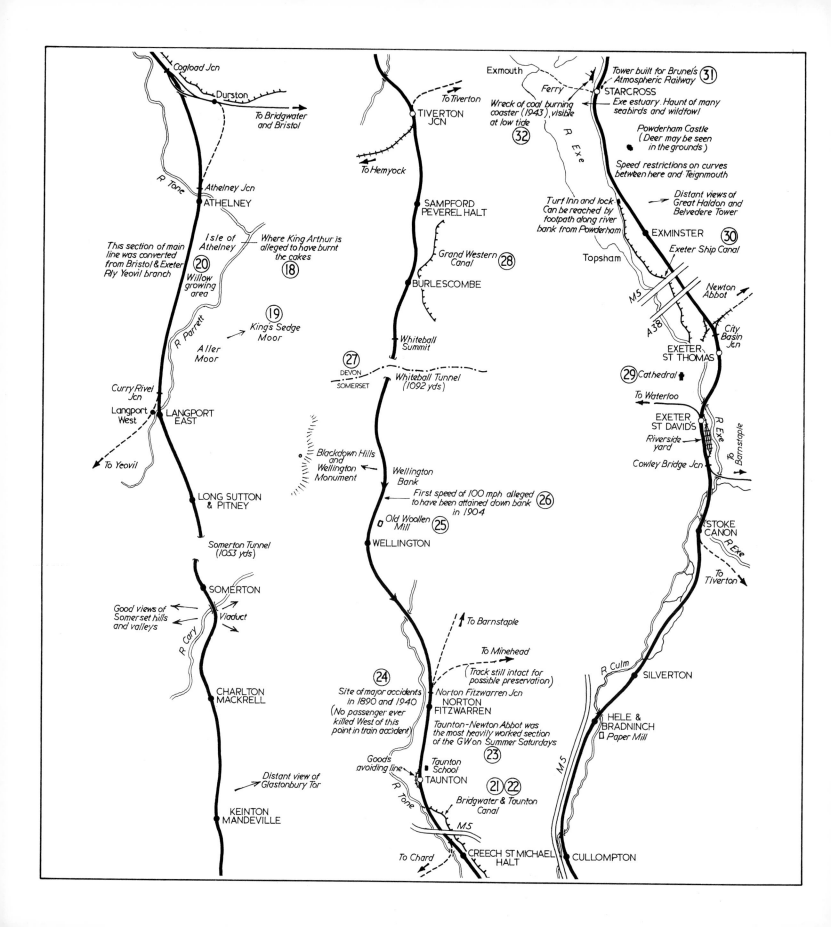

Cogload Jcn

Durston

To Bridgwater and Bristol

To Tiverton

TIVERTON JCN

To Hemyock

Exmouth

Ferry

Tower built for Brunel's Atmospheric Railway ㉛

STARCROSS

Wreck of coal burning coaster (1943), visible at low tide ㉜

Exe estuary. Haunt of many seabirds and wildfowl

Powderham Castle (Deer may be seen in the grounds)

R Exe

R Tone

Athelney Jcn

ATHELNEY

SAMPFORD PEVEREL HALT

Turf Inn and lock. Can be reached by footpath along river bank from Powderham

Distant views of Great Haldon and Belvedere Tower

Isle of Athelney

Where King Arthur is alleged to have burnt the cakes ⑱

EXMINSTER ㉚

Exeter Ship Canal

Topsham

Speed restrictions on curves between here and Teignmouth

This section of main line was converted from Bristol & Exeter Rly Yeovil branch ⑳

Grand Western Canal ㉘

BURLESCOMBE

Willow growing area

R Parrett

King's Sedge Moor ⑲

Aller Moor

Whiteball Summit

DEVON ㉗ SOMERSET

Whiteball Tunnel (1092 yds)

M5

A38

Newton Abbot

City Basin Jcn

EXETER ST THOMAS

Cathedral ㉙

Curry Rivel Jcn

Langport West

LANGPORT EAST

To Yeovil

Blackdown Hills and Wellington Monument

Wellington Bank

First speed of 100 mph alleged to have been attained down bank in 1904 ㉖

To Waterloo

EXETER ST DAVID'S

Riverside yard

Cowley Bridge Jcn

R Exe

To Barnstaple

LONG SUTTON & PITNEY

Old Woollen Mill ㉕

WELLINGTON

Somerton Tunnel (1053 yds)

SOMERTON

Good views of Somerset hills and valleys

Viaduct

R Cary

CHARLTON MACKRELL

Distant view of Glastonbury Tor

STOKE CANON

R Exe

To Tiverton

R Culm

SILVERTON

To Barnstaple

To Minehead

(Track still intact for possible preservation)

㉔

Site of major accidents in 1890 and 1940 (No passenger ever killed West of this point in train accident)

Norton Fitzwarren Jcn

NORTON FITZWARREN

Taunton-Newton Abbot was the most heavily worked section of the GW on Summer Saturdays ㉓

HELE & BRADNINCH

Paper Mill

M5

Goods avoiding line

Taunton School

TAUNTON

R Tone

㉑ ㉒

Bridgwater & Taunton Canal

M5

To Chard

CREECH ST MICHAEL HALT

CULLOMPTON

KEINTON MANDEVILLE

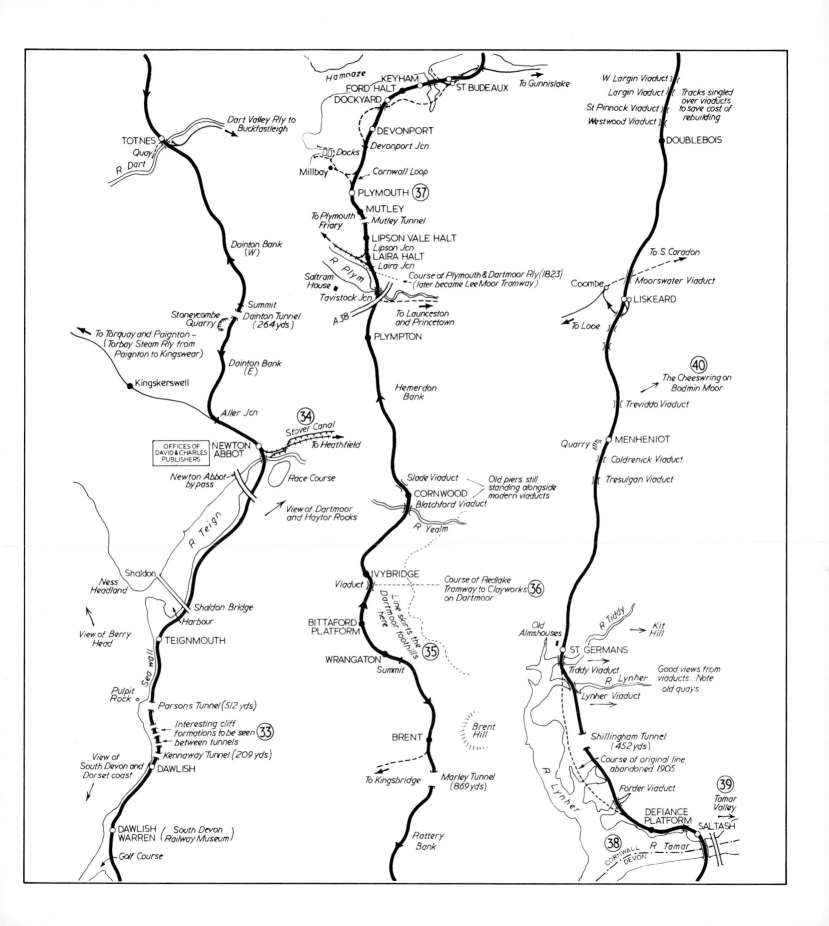

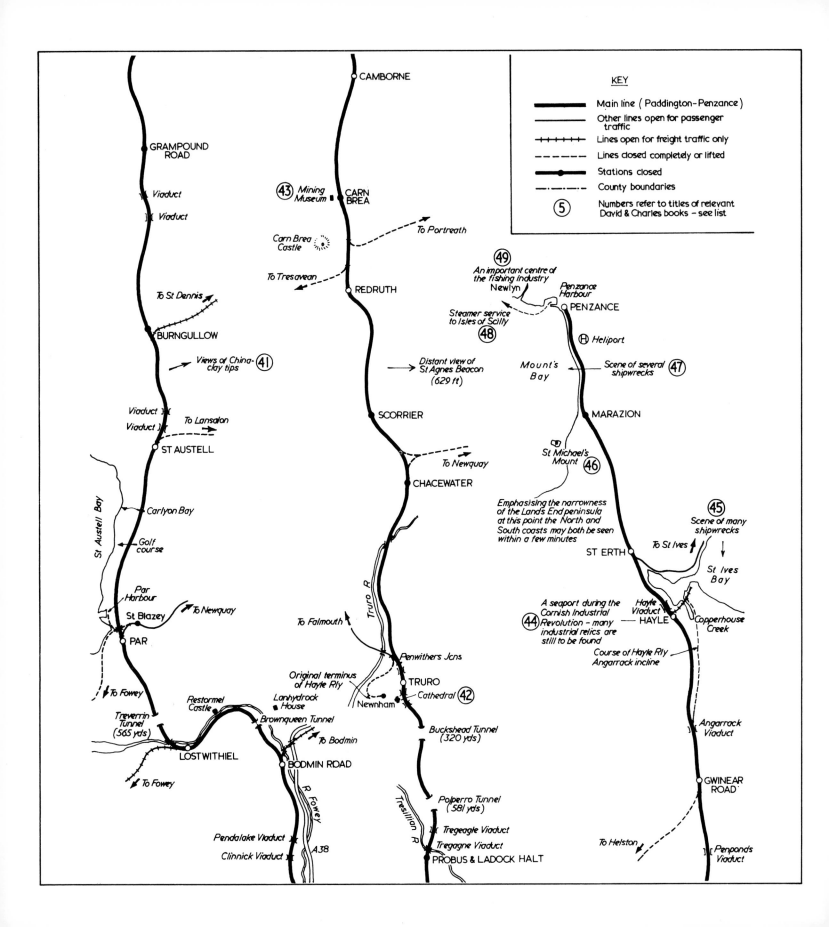

KEY

━━━ Main line (Paddington–Penzance)

──── Other lines open for passenger traffic

─+++─ Lines open for freight traffic only

─ ─ ─ Lines closed completely or lifted

━●━ Stations closed

─·─·─ County boundaries

(5) Numbers refer to titles of relevant David & Charles books – see list

CAMBORNE

GRAMPOUND ROAD

Viaduct

][Viaduct

(43) *Mining Museum* ■

CARN BREA

Carn Brea Castle

To Portreath

To Tresavean

REDRUTH

To St Dennis

BURNGULLOW

→ *Views of China-clay tips* (41)

(49) *An important centre of the fishing industry* Newlyn

Penzance Harbour

○ PENZANCE

Steamer service to Isles of Scilly (48)

Ⓗ *Heliport*

Distant view of St Agnes Beacon (629 ft)

Mount's Bay

Scene of several shipwrecks (47)

Viaduct][

Viaduct][

To Lansalon

○ ST AUSTELL

SCORRIER

MARAZION

St Michael's Mount (46)

St Austell Bay

Carlyon Bay

CHACEWATER

To Newquay

Emphasising the narrowness of the Land's End peninsula at this point the North and South coasts may both be seen within a few minutes

(45) *Scene of many shipwrecks*

Golf course

To St Ives

St Ives Bay

ST ERTH

Par Harbour

St Blazey ● → *To Newquay*

○ PAR

Truro R

To Falmouth

A seaport during the Cornish Industrial Revolution – many industrial relics are still to be found (44)

Hayle Viaduct

HAYLE ●

Copperhouse Creek

To Fowey

Restormel Castle ■

Treverrin Tunnel (565 yds)

Brownqueen Tunnel

Lanhydrock House ■

To Bodmin

Original terminus of Hayle Rly

Penwithers Jcns

○ TRURO (42)

Cathedral

Newnham

Course of Hayle Rly Angarrack incline

LOSTWITHIEL

To Fowey

BODMIN ROAD ●

R Fowey

Buckshead Tunnel (320 yds)

Angarrack Viaduct

Pendalake Viaduct ✕

Clinnick Viaduct ✕

A38

Tresillian R

Polperro Tunnel (581 yds)

To Helston

GWINEAR ROAD ○

Tregeagle Viaduct

Tregagne Viaduct

PROBUS & LADOCK HALT

Penpond's Viaduct ✕

Book List

The numbers on the maps on the previous pages relate to books published by David & Charles on subjects related to or visible from the railway between Paddington and Penzance. Below we give title and author. Other details, including price, may be obtained from our seasonal catalogue sent free on request. Several of the titles listed are temporarily out of print. For a general history of railways in South West England see book no 13.

BOOKS OF INTEREST RELATED TO THE LINE AND COUNTRYSIDE BETWEEN PADDINGTON AND PENZANCE

(key numbers relate to position on maps)

1 **London's Termini** Alan A. Jackson
2 **A Regional History of the Railways of Great Britain Vol 3 Greater London** H. P. White
3 **The GWR Stars, Castles and Kings Parts 1 and 2** O. S. Nock
4 **Diesel-Hydraulic Locomotives of the Western Region** Brian Reed
5 **Great Western Coaches 1890-1954** Michael Harris
6 **History of Great Western Goods Wagons Parts 1 and 2** A. Atkins, W. Beard, D. Hyde and R. Tourret
7 **The Canals of South and South East England** Charles Hadfield
8 **A Regional History of the Railways of Great Britain Vol 2 Southern England** H. P. White
9 **Holiday Cruising on the Thames** E. and P. W. Ball
10 **The London & South Western Railway Vols 1 and 2** R. A. Williams
11 **The Kennet & Avon Canal** K. R. Clew
12 **The Midland & South Western Junction Railway** Colin G. Maggs
13 **A Regional History of the Railways of Great Britain Vol 1 The West Country** David St John Thomas. Also available in paperback as **West Country Railway History**
14 **GWR Steam** O. S. Nock
15 **Great Western Progress 1835-1935** (Reprint of **Times** Centenary number)
16 **The Man Who Loves Giants An Artist Among Elephants and Engines** David Shepherd
17 **The Somerset & Dorset Railway** Robin Atthill
18 **Somerset Legends** Berta Lawrence
19 **Avalon & Sedgemoor** Desmond Hawkins. Also **Sedgemoor: Its History and Natural History** B. Storer
20 **Crafts from the Countryside** John L. Jones
21 **The Canals of South West England** Charles Hadfield
22 **British Canals** Charles Hadfield
23 **Summer Saturdays in the West** David St John Thomas and Simon Rocksborough Smith
24 **Red for Danger** (history of railway accidents) L. T. C. Rolt
25 **The Industrial Archaeology of Southern England** Kenneth Hudson
26 **Speed Records on Britain's Railways** O. S. Nock
27 **Devon** W. G. Hoskins
28 **The Grand Western Canal** Helen Harris
29 **Churches of Devon** J. M. Slader
30 **The Exeter Ship Canal** Kenneth R. Clew
31 **Atmospheric Railways** Charles Hadfield
32 **Devon Shipwrecks** Richard Larn
33 **Geology Explained in South and East Devon** John W. Perkins

For years before the outbreak of hostilities the Great Western had been planning for a mass evacuation from London.

Chronology

Paddington-Penzance opening dates

Section	Opening date (broad gauge)	Conversion to standard gauge
GW Paddington-Bristol line to Reading		
Paddington (original station)-Maidenhead (present Paddington opened 1854	4 June 1838	Mixed gauge 1861
Maidenhead-Twyford	1 July 1839	Broad-gauge rail removed 1892
Berks & Hants line (forms today's main line between Reading and Patney)		
Reading-Hungerford	21 December 1847	Standard gauge 1874
Hungerford-Devizes	11 November 1862	
Chippenham-Weymouth line (part of today's route between Westbury and Castle Cary		
Chippenham (Thingley Junction)-Westbury	5 September 1848	
Westbury-Frome	7 October 1850	Standard gauge 1874
Frome-Yeovil	1 September 1856	
Bristol & Exeter Railway Durston-Yeovil branch (part of today's route between Curry Rivel Junction and Athelney)		
Durston-Yeovil	1 October 1853	Mixed gauge 1867
		Broad-gauge rail removed 1879
Upgrading and new construction to make Berks & Hants line a through route		
Patney & Chirton-Westbury		29 July 1900
Castle Cary-Curry Rivel Junction		1905/6
Athelney-Cogload Junction		2 April 1906
Westbury avoiding line		1933
Frome avoiding line		1933
Bristol & Exeter Railway		
Bridgwater-Taunton	1 July 1842	Mixed gauge 1867/1875
Taunton-Beambridge	1 May 1843	Mixed gauge 1876
Beambridge-Exeter	1 May 1844	Broad-gauge rail removed 1892
The opening to Exeter in 1844 completed the through route between London and Exeter via Bristol		
South Devon Railway		
Exeter Teignmouth	30 May 1846	From Exeter to Penzance
Teignmouth-Newton Abbot (Atmospheric Traction 1847/8)	30 December 1846	broad and mixed gauge
Newton Abbot-Totnes	20 July 1847	track converted to standard
Totnes-Plymouth Laira	5 May 1848	gauge 1892
Plymouth Laira-Millbay	2 April 1849	
Cornwall Railway		
Plymouth-Truro	4 May 1859	
Truro-Penwithers Junction	11 May 1859	
West Cornwall Railway		
Truro Road-Penwithers Junction-Redruth	25 August 1855*	
Redruth-Penzance	11 March 1852*	

* As standard gauge. Broad-gauge rail added 1866

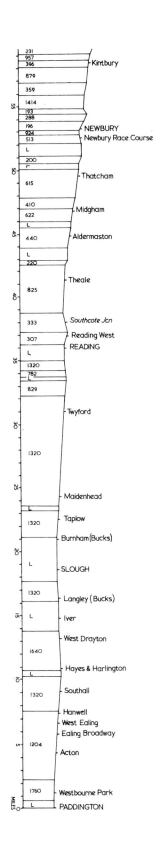
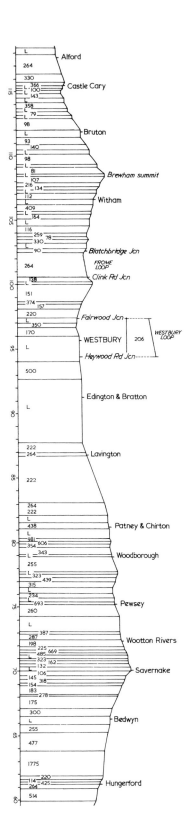
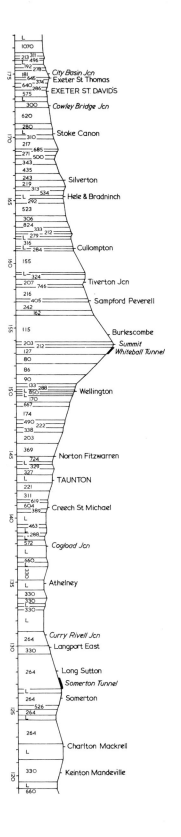

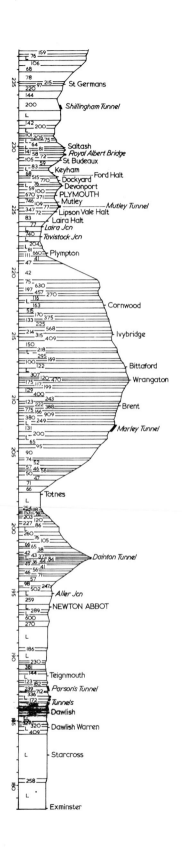

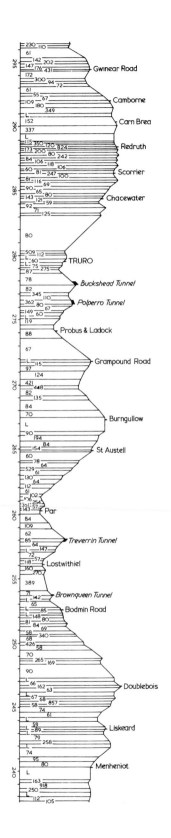

The gradient profile tells its own troubled story of the route's piecemeal development, parts of it originally as branch lines, as well as the difficult geography of the far West.

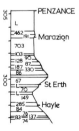

SOUTH DEVON RAILWAY.

PASSENGER TRAIN TABLE, 10TH MAY, 1859.

N.B. LONDON TIME, as regulated by the Guildhall Clock, Plymouth, is kept at all the Stations on the Railway:—it is 17 minutes earlier than PLYMOUTH and DEVONPORT time.

Distance (Miles)	UP TRAINS. From the day after the opening of the Cornwall Railway.	Week Days 1: 1&2 cl. Also 3 cl. to all S.D. statns. but not to the Exeter (B & E) Staton	Week Days 2: 1 & 2 class. Also 3 class to stations beynd Bath.	Week Days 3: Ex. Train 1 & 2 class.	Week Days 4: Mail to Bristol. 1 & 2 class.	Week Days 5: 1st, 2nd, and 3rd class.	Week Days 6: 1 & 2 cl. Also 3 cl from Plymth. to Plympton, Ivybridge, & Kingsbridge Road.	Week Days 7: 1st, 2nd, and 3rd class.	Week Days 8: Mail 1 & 2 class.	Sundays 1: 1, 2, 3 class	Sundays 2: Mail to Bristl. 1 & 2 class.	Sundays 3: 1, 2, 3 class.	Sundays 4: 1, 2, 3 class.	Sundays 5: Mail 1 & 2 class.
53½	TRURO, per Cornwall Railway		a.m. 5 45	a.m. 8 20		a.m. 11 0			p.m. 3 50		a.m. 6 50	..	..	p.m. 3 50
	TAVISTOCK													
	HORRABRIDGE													
	BICKLEIGH													
	PLYMOUTH													
		a.m.	a.m.	a.m.	noon.	p.m.	p.m.		p.m.	a.m.	noon.	p.m.		p.m.
	PLYMOUTH Departure	6 50	9 0	10 45	12 0	2 10	5 5	..	7 10	6 50	12 0	2 25		7 10
4½	PLYMPTON Arrival	7 2	9 12	..	12 15	2 22	5 17	..	7 22	7 2	12 15	2 37		7 22
9	CORNWOOD ROAD	7 17	..	..	..	2 37	*	..	..	7 17	..	2 52		..
11¼	IVYBRIDGE	7 23	9 30	..	12 35	2 44	5 37	..	7 42	7 23	12 35	2 59		7 42
14½	KINGSBRIDGE ROAD	7 32	9 39	11 15	12 45	2 52	5 45	..	7 50	7 32	12 45	3 7		7 50
17	BRENT	7 40	9 47	..	..	3 0	5 53	..	..	7 41	..	3 15		..
23¼	TOTNES	7 59	10 7	11 33	1 6	3 20	6 11	..	8 10	7 59	1 6	3 35		8 10
32¾	NEWTON Arrival	8 24	10 32	11 52	1 33	3 45	6 36	..	8 33	8 24	1 33	4 0		8 33
34¾	KINGSKERSWELL	..	10 45	12 5	..	..	6 45	..	..	8 35	..	..		..
37½	TORQUAY .... Arrival	..	10 55	12 15	..	4 15	6 55	..	..	8 45	..	4 20		..
	LIVERMEAD													
	PAIGNTON													
	BRIXHAM													
	DARTMOUTH													
	DARTMOUTH													
	CHURSTON FERRERS													
	PAIGNTON													
	LIVERMEAD													
	TORQUAY, Depar. for New.	7 40	10 10	11 30	1 5	3 30	6 15	7 15	..	8 5	..	3 40	7 15	..
2¾	KINGSKERSWELL	7 45	10 15	..	1 11	3 36	6 21	7 21	..	8 11	..	..	7 21	..
	NEWTON ......Departure	8 30	10 37	11 56	1 35	4 0	6 42	7 35	8 40	8 30	1 35	4 10	7 35	8 40
37¾	TEIGNMOUTH..Arrival	8 45	10 49	12 7	1 47	4 15	6 55	7 47	8 52	8 45	1 47	4 27	7 47	8 52
40¾	DAWLISH	8 57	11 0	12 16	1 57	4 27	7 5	7 57	9 2	8 57	1 57	4 37	7 57	9 2
44½	STARCROSS	9 10	11 10	12 25	2 7	4 42	7 17	8 7	9 12	9 10	2 7	4 47	8 7	9 12
48	EXMINSTER	9 20	..	..	..	4 52	..	8 17	..	9 20	..	4 57	8 17	..
51¼	ST. THOMAS (EXETER)	9 30	11 27	..	2 22	5 2	7 32	8 27	9 27	9 30	2 22	5 7	8 27	9 27
52¾	EXETER	9 40	11 35	12 45	2 30	5 10	7 40	8 35	9 35	9 40	2 30	5 15	8 35	9 35
128¾	BRISTOL fm. Br. & Ex. Rail.	12 40	3 45	2 45	5 30	8 50	11 0		12 25		5 20			12 25
246¾	PADDINGTON, from Great Western Railway	5 0	9 15	6 0	10 45	..			4 45		10 20			

FARES FROM PLYMOUTH.

Station	Ordinary Trains, Single Tickets, 1st class (s. d.)	Single, 2nd class (s. d.)	Single, 3rd class (s. d.)	Return Tickets, 1st class (s. d.)	Return, 2nd class (s. d.)	Return, 3rd class (s. d.)	Express Trains, Sin. Tickets, 1st class (s. d.)	Sin. Tickets, 2nd class (s. d.)	Ret. Tickets, 1st class (s. d.)	Ret. Tickets, 2nd class (s. d.)
TRURO	..	..	..	..	..	..	..	..	..	..
FARES FROM PLYMOUTH.										
PLYMOUTH	..	..	..	..	..	..	..	..	..	..
PLYMPTON	1 0	0 9	0 4½	1 4	1 0	0 8	..	..	..	..
CORNWOOD ROAD	1 10	1 5	0 9	2 2	1 7	1 0	..	..	..	..
IVYBRIDGE	2 5	1 9	0 11½	2 10	2 1	1 3	..	..	..	..
KINGSBRIDGE ROAD	3 1	2 3	1 2½	3 6	2 8	1 8	3 8	2 5	4 6	3 0
BRENT	3 6	2 7	1 5	4 0	3 2	2 0	..	..	..	..
TOTNES	5 1	3 7	1 11½	6 0	4 4	3 0	5 10	3 10	7 4	4 10
NEWTON	7 2	4 11	2 8½	8 10	5 10	..	8 0	5 3	10 0	6 6
KINGSKERSWELL	7 7	5 2	2 10½	9 0	6 2	..	..	..	..	..
TORQUAY	7 10	5 4	3 1½	9 6	6 10	..	8 10	5 10	11 0	7 6
FARES FROM TORQUAY.										
TORQUAY	..	..	..	..	..	..	..	..	..	..
KINGSKERSWELL	0 8	0 5	0 2½	1 0	0 8	..	..	..	..	..
FARES FROM PLYMOUTH.										
NEWTON	..	..	..	..	..	..	..	..	..	..
TEIGNMOUTH	8 4	5 8	3 1½	9 8	7 0	..	9 3	6 1	11 4	7 10
DAWLISH	9 0	6 1	3 4½	10 8	7 6	..	10 0	6 7	12 6	8 5
STARCROSS	9 8	6 7	3 8	11 8	8 2	..	10 11	7 2	13 7	9 2
EXMINSTER	10 5	7 2	4 0	12 7	8 10	..	..	..	..	..
ST. THOMAS (EXETER)	11 0	7 6	4 3½	13 6	9 6	7 0	..	..	..	..
EXETER	11 6	7 10	4 4½	14 2	9 10	7 10	13 0	8 6	16 6	11 0
BRISTOL	29 0	19 10	10 8	40 5	27 10		33 0	25 6	46 6	36 6
PADDINGTON	49 10	35 6	20 6	76 5	55 4		59 1	43 9	91 6	68 6

† *Passengers cannot be Booked to Up Trains from St. Thomas' Station.*

• *The 6.5 p.m. Up Train will stop at Cornwood Road on Tuesdays, Thursdays, and Saturdays, and 3rd Class Passengers will be Booked on these days from Plymouth to that Station.*

Table 5

Table 5

THE

ROYAL DUCHY

RESTAURANT CAR SERVICE

LONDON, EXETER, PLYMOUTH, TRURO and PENZANCE

WEEK DAYS

	E	S
	pm	pm
London (Paddington) .. .. ..dep	1A30	1A35
Reading General .. .. "	2U13	2U18
Westbury .. ..arr	3 18	3 26
Taunton .. .. "	4 13	4 25
Exeter (St. David's) .. .. .. "	4 53	5 5
Dawlish .. .. "	..	5 30
Teignmouth .. .. "	..	5 39
Newton Abbot .. .. "	5 27	5 50
Kingskerswell .. .. "	5 42	..
Torre .. .. "	5 50	..
Torquay .. .. "	5 53	..
Paignton .. .. "	6 6	..
Goodrington Sands Halt .. "	6 10	..
Churston (for Brixham) .. .. "	6 17	..
Kingswear .. .. "	6 27	..
Plymouth (North Road) .. .. "	6 25	6 55
Liskeard .. .. "	7 5	7 35
Bodmin Road .. .. "	7 21	7 50
Lostwithiel .. .. "	7 28	7 57
Par .. .. "	7 38	8 9
St. Austell .. .. "	7 49	8 20
Truro .. .. "	8 12	8 45
Chacewater .. .. "	..	9 0
Redruth .. .. "	8 33	9 10
Camborne .. .. "	8 42	9 18
Gwinear Road .. .. "	..	9 25
Hayle .. .. "	..	9 33
St. Erth .. .. "	8 57	9 38
Penzance .. .. "	9 10	9 55

	E	S
	am	am
Penzance .. ..dep	11A 0	11C50
Marazion .. .. "	..	11C54
St. Erth .. .. "	11A 9	12C 2
Camborne .. .. "	11A26	12C22
Redruth .. .. "	11A35	12C32
Chacewater .. .. "	11A43	..
	pm	
Truro .. .. "	12A 0	12 52
St. Austell .. .. "	12 26	1 22
Par .. .. "	12 35	..
Lostwithiel .. .. "	12 47	1 40
Bodmin Road .. .. "	12 56	..
Liskeard .. .. "	1 17	2 8
Plymouth (North Road) .. .. "	2 0	2 50
Kingswear .. .. "	1B50	..
Churston (for Brixham) .. .. "	2B 0	..
Paignton .. .. "	2B 9	..
Torquay .. .. "	2B18	..
Torre .. .. "	2T22	..
Newton Abbot .. .. "	2 55	..
Teignmouth .. .. "	2T46	..
Dawlish .. .. "	2T55	..
Exeter (St. David's) .. .. .. "	3 30	..
Taunton .. .. "	4 14	..
Westbury .. .. "	5 14	..
Newbury .. ..arr	6 2	6 38
Reading General .. .. "	6 25	7 1
London (Paddington) .. .. .. "	7 15	7 50

A—Seats can be reserved in advance on payment of a fee of 2s. 0d. per seat (see page 22).
B—Mondays to Thursdays only. Note A also applies
C—Passengers travelling by this train beyond Plymouth are required to hold Regulation Tickets (see page 31)
E—Except Saturdays
S—Saturdays only
T—Mondays to Thursdays only
U—Calls to take up passengers only

54

Table 6

Table 6

THE MAYFLOWER

RESTAURANT CAR SERVICE

LONDON, TAUNTON, EXETER, NEWTON ABBOT and PLYMOUTH

WEEK DAYS

	pm
London (Paddington) ... ...dep	5A30
Taunton ... ...arr	7 57
Exeter (St. David's)... ... ... "	8 37
Dawlish ... ... "	9 7
Teignmouth ... ... "	9 15
Newton Abbot ... ... "	9 25
Torre ... ... "	9 39
Torquay ... ... "	9 42
Paignton ... ... "	9 53
Churston (for Brixham) ... "	10 5
Kingswear ... ... "	10 15
Plymouth (North Road) ... "	10 0

	E	S
	am	am
Plymouth (North Road) dep	8A30	8A30
Kingswear ... ... "	8A30	...
Churston (for Brixham) "	8A40	...
Paignton ... ... "	8A50	...
Torquay ... ... "	8A58	...
Torre ... ... "	9 3	...
Newton Abbot ... ... "	9 26	...
Exeter (St. David's) ... "	10 0	9 57
Taunton ... ... "	10 40	10 40
Westbury ... ... "	11 40	11 40
	pm	pm
Reading General ... ...arr	12C45	12D47
London (Paddington) ...."	1 25	1 35

A—Seats can be reserved in advance on payment of a fee of 2s. 0d. per seat (see page 22).
C—Slip Carriage (Restaurant Car not available).
D—Calls to set down passengers only.
E—Except Saturdays. S—Saturdays only.

53

VIA PLYMOUTH TO AND FROM HAVRE

By the FRENCH LINE (Cie Gle Transatlantique).

Regular Sailings by New York and West Indian Liners calling at Plymouth on homeward and outward voyages.

Local passengers are carried to and from France at cheap fares. Through tickets from the principal G.W. Rly. Stations.

VIA PLYMOUTH TO BORDEAUX

By the French Line's West Indian Liners calling at Bordeaux *en route* to West Indies.

Further particulars can be obtained at the Offices of the French Line (Compagnie Générale Transatlantique), 22, Pall Mall, S.W.1, or from Mr. R. H. Nicholls, Superintendent of the Line, Paddington Station, W.2.

Top a South Devon Railway handbill. Middle, in the late 1950s the Western Region was given authority to reintroduce the traditional Great Western's chocolate-and-cream livery for the coaches of named trains. The number of named trains then quickly multiplied. This extract is from the Western Region timetable of summer 1958 when restaurant cars still ran through to Penzance and Reading was still served by slip coach off the time-honoured 8.30am from Plymouth. Bottom. The Great Western's 1928 timetable advertising Plymouth services.

Acknowledgements

Photographs are acknowledged with thanks from the following sources:

Donald R. Barber

British Railways, Western Region

D. E. Canning

K. Connolly

Michael Dadley

R. H. Darlaston

S. Desbrow

T. G. Flinders

P. J. Fowler

G. F. Gillham

P. W. Gray

C. S. Heaps

G. F. Heiron

R. W. Hinton

Derek Jones

Locomotive and General Railway Photographs

G. A. Richardson

R. F. Roberts

Gerald T. Robinson

J. R. Smith

R. E. Toop

K. J. Vincent

T. E. Williams

The plan of Paddington station is reproduced from *London's Termini* where it was used by permission of the *Railway Magazine*. Maps drawn by Vic Welch. Finally, thanks to all who have given help, especially Geoffrey Kichenside, Judith Wyles and my wife Pamela.